D1112484

BLAMING CHINA

BLAMING CHINA

It Might Feel Good but It
Won't Fix America's Economy

BENJAMIN SHOBERT

POTOMAC BOOKS | *An imprint of the University of Nebraska Press*

Library of Congress Cataloging-in-Publication Data
Names: Shobert, Benjamin, author.
Title: Blaming China: it might feel good but it won't
fix America's economy / Benjamin Shobert.
Description: Lincoln: Potomac Books, [2018] |
Includes bibliographical references and index.
Identifiers: LCCN 2018009202
ISBN 9781612349954 (cloth: alk. paper)
ISBN 9781640121195 (epub)
ISBN 9781640121201 (mobi)
ISBN 9781640121218 (pdf)
Subjects: LCSH: United States—Economic
conditions—21st century. | United States—Foreign
economic relations—China. | China—Foreign
economic relations—United States.
Classification: LCC HC106.83 .S56 2018
DDC 330.973—dc23 LC record available at
https://lccn.loc.gov/2018009202

Set in Sabon Next by Mikala R Kolander.
Designed by N. Putens.

"America's problem is not that it does not work like China. It is that it no longer works like America."

—RICHARD MCGREGOR, Washington bureau chief of the *Financial Times*

CONTENTS

PREFACE

Bringing your first book to market is a daunting experience. In my case, the process began nearly five years ago, when in the period after the 2008 financial crisis, I began to sense that something was going sour in the United States. Having grown up in the American Midwest, where uncertainties about globalization, in particular how it would impact working-class blue-collar families, were particularly acute, and at the same time having spent a good part of my adult life working across emerging economies (with China in particular), I began to wonder if the U.S. lack of confidence in its future could lead toward war with China. While the idea of war with China was not new, the idea that America—unmoored, anxious, and beset by a variety of economic, political, and national security dysfunctions— could be the cause of such a conflict was a disruptive idea.

As the presidential election of 2016 ended, I was certainly not alone in the belief that something had gone badly wrong in American life. It was widely acknowledged that the United States was deeply unmoored from its values, open to violating long-standing norms that had ensured our country stood as an object lesson to the world for what it meant to be a functioning republic. Say what any of us might about President Donald Trump; being angry at him, or his voters, misses the point and likely only makes things worse. Trump reflects something essential and true about America's insecurities right now, something our best pundits and politicians have failed to preempt. Many of those who are now aghast at his presidency have for too long harbored a false sense of superiority and profound detachment from the needs of average Americans. Most worrisome to me was seeing him direct American insecurities toward an outside actor, China, as the cause of America's problems. I believe that his emphasis on China as the source of many American economic anxieties is the beginning of a process that will lead Americans to blame China for problems for which we have only ourselves to blame, a process that could easily spiral out of control and take both countries down the path toward war.

I did not write this book for China policy wonks. I wrote this book for the businessman, the current events reader, the concerned citizen who shares my sense that America has forgotten what its political system is supposed to deliver for the average American family. I wrote this book in the hopes it would reach parts of popular culture where a bit of honest self-reflection on America's problems can be useful, before the discussion about China accelerates, becomes more negative and volatile, and destabilizes the world. Nothing in this book assumes that China has it all figured out or that, as some authors have suggested, America should emulate China; in fact, having traveled and worked in a variety of developed and emerging markets around the world, I would rather play America's hand than that of any other country. Our economic, demographic, political, and cultural problems pale in comparison to those faced by western Europe or China. We have every reason to believe that another hundred years of peace and prosperity await us, but only if we avoid blaming China and instead focus on those structural reforms that need to be made, reforms that will inevitably violate long-held beliefs of both Democrats and Republicans. As alarmist as it may seem, what seems more likely to you, the reader? That American politics will rediscover its center and double down on policies designed to help the working class, or that an inept American Congress and presidency will lurch toward war with a competing global power?

The political choices and the intentional ill will that has been fed and directed between citizens of the United States will at some point escalate and require an outside actor against which to direct that ill will. I write this in the hopes that America can disengage from a path I see leading to war, a path that will cost the lives of many whom I love and call family and friend. I am especially concerned that these same people, who I know are perfectly decent and well intentioned, have in an act of careless politics and rabid ideology ushered in a moment that will ask the ultimate sacrifice of them and their children. Political choices have consequences, ones that too few Americans have been asked to share in over two decades of war in Afghanistan and Iraq. It is unlikely the next war of choice America initiates will ask as little of the American family as the two most recent ones have.

I have many people to thank for their support and feedback as I wrote this book, and only myself to blame for the errors, omissions, and incomplete thoughts. No one has been more supportive throughout this entire process than my wife, Jennifer. The decision to write a book for the first time, the process of editing it, finding an agent, and going through the publication process were not easy, and she was my biggest supporter the entire time. Wrestling with the ideas in this book has not been without its ups and downs, and many an evening has been occupied either with the work of writing or with the mental burden of the thoughts themselves. She has always given me the space and support I need and the love I cherish but do not always deserve.

Any number of people have provided assistance to me in this process. I owe a special debt of thanks to my dear friend Damjan Denoble, who was a special sort of sounding board and encouraging voice. Life has a special way of bringing just the right people into your life at just the right time, and Damjan was definitely one such person. Claire Topal was a perfect cheerleader when I needed one, and her energy and enthusiasm is something I very much appreciate. Dere Newman, who will likely disagree with much of what I write here, was a faithful supporter and provided me room to write when this project was first leaping off a white board and into an outline. She will always be someone I am thankful to have had in my life. Friends like Dan Harris, Kurt Rosenberg, Marc Szepan, Bill Gulledge, and Eric Lee are each, in their own way, people who offered important personal support as I wrote this book. I am thankful to each of them in unique ways and hope that I am as good a friend to them as they have been to me. I am thankful for Jill Marsal, who took a chance on me as my agent, and Jill Jago, who helped edit. As must always be said, the misstatements and inaccuracies that remain are entirely my fault.

And so, with these thanks in mind, let us begin this journey, an exploration into how a country that the United States once could afford to be generous to, one we successfully brought our way and triangulated against in opposition to the Soviet Union, has now become a problem we believe must be addressed. Americans tend to view history as something that happens outside our borders, something we can observe at a safe distance and, should we choose to get involved, emerge on the right side of. But the events of the 2016 presidential election were different. This historical moment is us; it is here; it is now. The consequences of what follows will not be felt only in some faraway land; these consequences will visit America's shores.

Hubris has led Americans to believe that politics does not matter, that our form of government is so well designed that it could never succumb to the same cancers and ossification that have affected other great nations before us.

Our country's relative safety and well-being has made us cavalier about the need for competent leadership, good government, a responsible media, and mindful politics. It has been too long since our politics cost each and every one of us something precious. Too many of the sacrifices our political ideas ask of us have been born by too few. That ended in the 2016 election.

What comes next will be a brutal reminder that politics most definitely matters. What comes next is a cold hard reality in which multipolar worlds, bereft of clear hegemons to constrain regional conflict, lurch toward war. What comes next is an economic reset that will upend the modern era of globalization and leave multinationals, industrial agriculture, and capital with fewer markets to access.

What comes next is an unconstrained form of conservative politics that will test its laissez-faire worldview in tax policy, health care, regulations, environmental protections, education, and foreign policy. What comes next is an unmoored postmodern liberal politics that uses identity politics rather than the vocal advocation of policies that reminds everyone that politics is designed to balance the needs of the individual against those of the whole.

What comes next is the logical conclusion of a nearly century-old methodical attempt to tear down post-Enlightenment political systems, philosophy, and scientific inquiry.

What comes next is fear of the other as the animating force in American life.

Politics doesn't matter. Until it does. And it does now.

BLAMING CHINA

1

Afraid of China? Maybe You Should Be

"China was globalization's tipping point, beyond which there is only further integration or war."

—Tom Barnett, author of *Great Powers* and *The Pentagon's New Map*

In late June of 2016, Donald Trump's campaign saw fit to hold its first major economic and trade speech in front of a pile of garbage. What flowed from the candidate's mouth would have been, twenty years ago, widely derided by people on both sides of the aisle. Now, it seems strangely relevant, a realization that should worry everyone. President Donald Trump represents the line of thinking that has always been ascendant when past eras of globalization came to an end: that free trade in some way disadvantages businesses and workers in developed markets, and as such, barriers must be constructed.

Over the last several years I have wondered what our world would look like if China were not a part of it. Not from the perspective of a consumer; rather, what would our world look like if China had not opened after Nixon's historic trip? Would China have become a dysfunctional cousin to the Soviet Union? Would it be a much bigger version of North Korea, except with a billion hungry mouths to feed rather than Pyongyang's millions? Would China be using its nuclear arsenal in ways even more destabilizing to the world than North Korea does? What would the globalized world, which many of us take for granted, look like without China?

Given how Republican president Donald Trump has spoken about China, it would seem Americans wish China had stayed poor, isolated, and powerless. For elites in Washington DC on both sides of the aisle up until the 2016 election, this was all noise, but to politically disenfranchised and economically dislocated middle-class Americans, blaming China for our economic problems had been embraced as truth. As is almost always the case, the people were ahead of the politicians. Trump channeled these anxieties perfectly toward China, saying in the heat of the 2015 presidential primary, "When was the last time anybody saw us beating, let's say, China in a trade deal? They kill us."[1] As the American economy has struggled to create wins for more than those who are already wealthy, politicians have become increasingly willing to point toward China as the party to blame for the pervasive insecurities that have come to define too much of American political life.

Not too long ago, these would have been ridiculous thoughts to hear from American politicians, but no longer. Largely absent from America's discussion in popular culture about trade with China today is the idea that both win by trading with one another. Now trade is perceived to be a zero-sum game, where China's win is America's loss. This leads to an important question: is America's frustration with China nothing more than a distraction from profound insecurities the United States has about its economy, global status, and domestic politics? If so, then is it possible America will decide to act on this blame game toward China rather than wrestling with problems wholly our making?

During trips to Washington DC to attend various congressional hearings and participate in think tank discussions on China, I have heard many angry comments about China, specifically how its economic gain has been at the cost of American jobs. Always in the background were fears about whether China could really be trusted; after all, they are still a "Communist" country. We have witnessed a variety of public intellectuals put out new books that have challenged long-held ideas about why an open and engaged China was ultimately good for the United States. Such thought leaders as James Mann in his book *The China Fantasy: How Our Leaders Explain Away Chinese Oppression* went back and questioned the most basic assumptions about whether China would develop into something similar to a Western democracy or become a more wealthy authoritarian government hostile to American values and potentially competing with our military for supremacy.

Today, the United States and China are moving toward a fundamental repositioning of their relations, a repositioning as significant as when Nixon went to China. When Donald Trump called the Trans-Pacific Partnership (TPP) a "rape of our country," he channeled the raw feelings of many blue-collar American workers who felt the elites have marginalized the needs of the working man over those of business and the 1 percent.[2] Trump is not alone. Democratic presidential candidate Bernie Sanders echoed similar criticisms when asked about his own thoughts on globalization: "Let's be clear: one of the major reasons that the middle class in America is disappearing, poverty is increasing and the gap between the rich and everyone else is growing wider and wider is due to our disastrous unfettered free-trade policy."[3] And what of the 2016 Democratic nominee for president and former secretary of state Hillary Clinton? Her own position on trade, and on the TPP specifically, was convoluted and, at the twilight of her ill-fated campaign, hostile.[4] Her tortured attempts to walk back her prior advocacy for TPP reflected not only her own lack of conviction and attempts at political expediency, they also spoke to how far right the Democratic Party had moved on trade, largely the result of policies Clinton's husband had successfully advocated for in the nineties.

Beyond the venom of the 2016 presidential campaign, in private, congressmen who should know better refer to China as "Reds" or "Communists" with too much venom to be a simple slip of the tongue. In public, others such as Republican congressman Dana Rohrabacher from California are all too eager to feed the flames. Showing real insight into how many Americans already viewed China, in 2012 Rohrabacher opposed foreign aid to China on the congressional floor with an impassioned plea to remind his colleagues that "43 cents of every dollar we spend is borrowed money and Communist China is the single largest foreign holder of U.S. debt."[5] What Rohrabacher lacks in subtlety he makes up for in understanding how to connect with the voters in his district and others spread across America. Ideas about China's ultimate liberalization, the good it has done for everyone by serving as the world's factory, or its needs as a still-developing economy are no longer the predominant and accepted perspectives on the country. Now a much simpler and more dangerous line of thinking has evolved: China's gains are America's losses, and these gains must be stopped. Stopped to protect the American middle class. Stopped to ensure America's global military hegemony. Stopped to reinforce the belief that only America's political system is the standard against which every country should model itself.

The United States needs a reminder on why China matters while we all reflect on the reality that the American political establishment squandered the opportunity to help the average American as the twin pressures of globalization and automation began to mount. Without this reminder, America could upset much that has proven capable and trustworthy in stabilizing the world over the past several decades. The easy avenue for American policy is to blame China for problems of our own making, but doing so would distract Americans from the substantial changes we need to make at home, changes that have nothing to do with our relationship toward China. The more fixated we become on China as the source of our problems, the more likely a future politician even more manipulative than Donald Trump will distract us by blaming China, with the real potential of global conflict in the balance. Blaming China is not only shortsighted; it will do nothing to remedy America's economic problems. In fact, blaming China for our own mistakes could sow the seeds for an unnecessary trade war and military conflict.

Groups of Democratic politicians see China as a threat to one of their most traditional constituencies: labor unions who fear even more job losses from Chinese competition. Parts of the Republican Party share similar grievances. In addition, large segments of Republicans distrust China's leaders and hold misgivings based on the country's Communist past. Consequently, members of Congress are particularly uncomfortable with China's military buildup and its regional aspirations in relation to Taiwan and the South China Sea. Steve Bannon, the Trump administration's former chief strategist, stated this bluntly in 2016: "We're going to war in the South China Sea in five to 10 years. . . . There's no doubt about that. They're taking their sandbars and making basically stationary aircraft carriers and putting missiles on those. They come here to the United States in front of our face—and you understand how important face is—and say it's an ancient territorial sea."[6] Any number of Republicans like Bannon and his ilk have a serious hangover from the Cold War and appear too comfortable with finally having another competitor to drop into the preordained spot the Soviet Union had formerly occupied. Both Democrats and Republicans harbor concerns about China's human rights record and the various market access issues that have begun to sour the business community's ideas about China as a potential market. The storm clouds are gathering for anyone with the humility to really listen to the many anxieties of the American public that President Trump has tapped into, insecurities that pulse and inflame with every layoff, political failure, and terrorist attack. The message is simple: these things have happened because America is weak, and only belligerent strength will make America great again.

Attitudes toward China are also influenced by 9/11. The shapeless and largely stateless nature of terrorism makes it the sort of threat governments are ill equipped to deal with. While militant Islam remains a competitive political ideology and worldview in some of the same ways as Soviet- and Chinese-style Communism was, militant Islam remains an asymmetric threat that leaves America's political and military institutions without responses that satisfy the American electorate. As the West's frustration over how to deal with the ambiguous nature of terrorism grows, so too does the possibility that we will look for a conventional state against which to project our fears and frustrations in a misplaced attempt to make ourselves feel safe. Where global jihad is amorphous, China is a nation-state with an actual government, opposing ideology, and growing power against which America can define itself.

The last Bush administration intentionally tapped into a similar vein and produced one of the original arguments that led us into Iraq. In the months following 9/11, a tenuous relationship between state-sponsored terrorism and Iraqi president Saddam Hussein was enough to get Americans to support an invasion of Iraq. The insecurities and desire to do *something* led us to misperceive that country as a threat. Similar anxieties could also lead us to the same type of miscalculations regarding China but with even more disastrous possibilities. As a consequence of China's Communist past and socialist present, the country presents Washington with a state-on-state ideological counterpoint and potential (if yet imaginary) threat. China can be understood through many of the conventional Cold War prisms our leaders are most comfortable using to set national policy. It would be a mistake to underestimate the potential for conflict between the United States and China, if for no other reason than the ease with which China can be slipped into the uninspired thinking of a political class in Washington possessed of its own insecurities: governing citizens who find themselves in a particularly sour mood.

Regardless of the other ideological incompatibilities between the two parties in Washington, large segments from both sides agree that China's economic policies are problems for American business. Both want more aggressive trade remedies. This might not seem like a big adjustment, but it is. When past tensions around free trade accords flared up, China could count on a strong business community broadly supported by both Democrats and Republicans to push back against dissenting voices, as happened during the negotiation to grant China most favored nation status or to allow China's entry into the World Trade Organization (WTO).

But Trump's election has sent two messages to America's politicians. First, ramping up rhetoric about China pays dividends. Second, rhetoric against China is not going to be enough. The time for action against China is coming. China has watched the 2016 election with equal parts concern and bemusement: concern over the possibility that its largest trading partner is clearly moving toward a more hostile view of China, bemusement over the vessel the American people have entrusted to remedy America's perceived issues with China, someone particularly susceptible to a type of flattery that China's more sophisticated leaders easily recognize. America now finds itself negotiating with China from a position of perceived weakness, which the Chinese are acutely aware of. Trump channeled this insecurity in his June 2016 trade policy speech when he asserted, "China respects strength and by letting them take advantage of us economically, which they are doing like never before, we have lost all of their respect."[7]

The world may wait this all out, trusting that America's political and economic institutions will again find their footing and that China will develop a clearer understanding of what its trade partners expect in terms of economic openness and the need for further political liberalization. But the world is atomizing along long-dormant lines of nationalism, tribalism, economics, and governing philosophies. Those who believe in globalization and that staying connected to China is therefore good and necessary are now challenged to go back and convince others, to cover ground that many older China hands in particular feel is old and well worn. On the off chance that this moment in time is different because of America's insecurities, it must again be proven, using the most current facts, why blaming China is a dead end. In addition, a clear and compelling vision of a future in which China and the United States can compete but peacefully coexist is sorely needed.

Americans are victors of the Cold War, advocates and enablers of globalization, and progenitors of the Internet revolution. Yet we are unsure how to greet today's new economic realities or what policies best advance our own economic priorities. Over the last thirty years, major shifts in the global economy have largely been to our advantage. On the rare occasion when a recession buffeted America's shores, concerns over jobs shipped overseas or a struggling manufacturing sector would present themselves, but these concerns would dissipate once the economy regained its footing. Since 9/11 Americans have been disquieted on multiple fronts: the 9/11 attacks themselves, the 2008 great financial crisis, the multiple domestic political crises with no resolutions. They have all taken their toll on the American psyche. Everyone hopes the 2016 president election will have been the moment when our collective fever breaks, but it may well point to a fundamentally broken political system that no longer has the flexibility or stamina to wrestle with issues of any complexity. If that is the case, then America likely stands at the forefront of a new chapter in its history, one marked by a profound sense of loss and misplaced anger.

To say that Americans are feeling insecure at this moment would be an understatement. We bring this to bear in our view of every domestic or international issue, and our relationship with China is no different. This charged environment has been challenged by multiple story lines over the last several years that have only escalated tensions between the United States and China: China's massive cyber-spying programs, its enormous share of American treasuries, multiple American companies' announcements that China had infiltrated their corporate networks, China's handling of dissenting political voices, and China's military buildup. The accumulation of all of this has bent Americans toward a more hostile view of what it means to call China a partner. A 2014 poll by the Chicago Council on Foreign Affairs illustrated this point. They found that "only 33 percent of Americans encourage developing stronger ties with China."[8]

We have taken for granted that everyone understands and agrees why China matters to the United States. Does this country, once deemed so critical to our foreign policy, once a counterweight to the Soviet Union, no longer matter? Can China no longer be viewed as someone we could work with in pursuit of common goals? Can China accumulate power without America losing it? And perhaps most important, if we can no longer view China in a constructive light, where does that leave us: are we enemies? If so, can anyone envision a future with an economic equivalent to the Cold War? Is globalization rejected in such a world? And if globalization is destroyed, what does our world look like? Even worse, are we beginning to view China as America's existential threat, a country that embodies a threat to core parts of how we understand the American experience, going all the way back to the Revolutionary War, when China does little more than reflect the inadequacies of our own political economy?

Are we overlooking the potential for our once-stable world to come apart at the seams? In my home library is a thoroughly highlighted copy of Norman Angell's *The Great Illusion*. Angell, an early 1900s British historian, wrote two versions of this book, one in 1913 and one in 1933. His premise was that nations should understand the folly of war as a means to increase their national treasury. He believed this would make war less likely, with stability the remaining order of the day. Only when survivors surveyed the wreckage in the aftermath of two world wars could it be said he had twice been proven disastrously wrong.

Consider the warnings implicit in David Fromkin's book *Europe's Last Summer: Who Started the Great War in 1914?*. Fromkin covered the cause of the First World War, a war he suggests surprised the citizens of Europe as they returned home from summer holiday:

> The wars were about power. Specifically, they were about relative ranking among the Great European powers that at the time ruled most of the world. *Both Germany and Austria believed themselves to be on the way down. Each started a war in order to stay where it was* ... Although soldiers in the trenches for the four long years beginning in 1914 came to believe that the war was pointless, that was not so. It was about the most important issue in politics: who should rule the world. [emphasis added][9]

Conflict, yes, even war, surprises us when it should not. History is full of great wars that came as a shock to the average person but were later proven to be the work of manipulative politicians who believed a war would provide them some short-term gain. As improved as today's more enlightened man might be, he is still represented by politicians who many times seek to demonize others for problems they lack the courage or wisdom to address themselves. When leaders are found to be feckless and bereft of ideas, everyone looks for someone to blame. In a time of crisis, most politicians possess an appetite for remedies that, in times of greater prosperity and security, would be easily recognized as imprudent. Fromkin's words have something to say about the limitations of our political class today. We have too many politicians who, being aware of America's problems and feeling impotent to stop them, may look toward a confrontation with China now, when America has a lead, in order to halt China's accumulation of power. Such a push would also distract Americans from the inadequacies of their own government.

Even the most constructive thinkers about China's role in the future have expressed reservations. Dr. Thomas Barnett, one such thinker, referenced this possibility in a 2008 article of *Good Magazine* where he wrote, "China's decision to rejoin the world was globalization's tipping point, meaning—absent global war—there's no turning back now, only adaption."[10] While no one wants to believe that conflict with China is inevitable, it remains a real possibility unless we find new reasons to avoid blaming China for problems we have created. Instead, we must challenge ourselves to do better by first and foremost focusing on changes America needs to make.

If China cannot transition from a poor and isolated country to become a part of the global order as it currently is, then much of the modern era's beliefs about globalization and the inherent superiority of the capitalist model is broken. Unlike what such politicians as Clinton, Sanders, and Trump have put forward, a schism with China would not only damage free trade but would also call into question whether the American model of democracy is in fact superior to competing ideas about government, such as the model China has. In his seminal study of politics, historian Alan Ryan points out that China's form of government may owe more to Plato's ideas about the role of government than to those of Confucius. Ryan wryly notes, "[Plato could argue] as a flatly sociological proposition that a polis—or a modern state—functions best when there is a clear class structure with powerless workers, a military caste that knows its business, and an educated governing class whose right to rule is taken for granted. It would not be impossible to present modern China as evidence in favor of the thought."[11] Americans seem to have forgotten that for our approach to politics to be superior to China's, our economic and political systems must create better outcomes for our people than China's model has delivered for theirs. Whether or not American politicians did what was needed to prepare American workers for how China's entry would impact the American middle class in particular is critical to this question. If this is not how an impoverished and politically backward country can modernize, then what is the alternative? This does not presume that China should be forever treated with kid gloves or that China's model is somehow uniquely superior to the American model. Nor does it suggest that the world should give China a pass on the many social and environmental problems it perpetuates.

Troubling problems exist within China that cannot be overlooked. The country's leadership remains distrustful of its own people. Beijing disagrees with America's beliefs on the rights and responsibilities of government and individuals. At America's best, our governing principles reflect battles hard-fought during the European Enlightenment, when ideas about individual freedom and liberty were made accessible to all, and institutions were designed to protect both. Our two countries still have extreme differences in how we view the role of dissent in governing. China's heavy-handed response to domestic dissent reflects not only insecurity by its ruling party but also a deep ideological disagreement between China and the United States that cannot be forever trivialized.

Similarly, no one should downplay the environmental damage being done in China. America's growth occurred very much in tandem with modern industrialization. The United States had the advantage of modernizing at the same time it gradually expanded into a frontier characterized by vast expanses of sparsely occupied and highly arable land. We made our own mistakes, polluted our own rivers, and ravaged our own land, not to mention displacing the Native American population and looking the other way as to slavery while doing so. China does not have this luxury: its embrace of industrialization has occurred so quickly and at such a magnitude that it has not always been able to avoid major environmental problems that impact not only its own country but the world's ecology as well.

The central question remains: why must America avoid blaming China? First, because the world has no alternative method for bringing a reclusive, isolated, and dysfunctional country from near-starvation to a growing economy than to encourage trade with such countries as China, with the small set of comparative advantages it has. For China its initial offering to the world's economy came in the form of inexpensive labor; later, access to the massive unexplored Chinese market became further incentive for bilateral trade. If China is not going to be accommodated in this way, it is more because of America's own insecurities and fear of change than a flaw in the ideas that opened China up to the West. Our frustrations with China are misplaced. China is, in the most real sense, a mirror for Americans to see our own inadequacies. We see in our lost jobs that we have not created new opportunities for the working American. We see in Chinese holdings of American treasuries no illicit goal on China's part but instead an out-of-control American government unable to live within its means. The right path forward is not to blame China. Rather, we should work toward a more capable and competent political economy focused on what we must prioritize to have a better future.

To support this, it is critical to begin with an introduction to the ideas about China of the two quite different camps in America: Dragon Slayers, who believe China is a threat and must be beaten back, and Panda Huggers, who believe China is working to reform itself and can ultimately be trusted. These two views are on a collision course not only because of China but also because they represent a level of political dysfunction in the United States that has resulted in an environment in which blaming China is becoming the cheap answer to an expensive problem: namely, the inability and unwillingness of America's political class to acknowledge the hard choices that must be made to improve the lives of families across America. In addition, this book will briefly look back at China's most recent history, which should help Americans understand just how desperate the situation in China has been for most of the last century. Seeing this should help everyone understand how far China has come toward the changes we have asked of them. Finally, we will explore four major American insecurities—about our economics, our politics, our shifting status as a world power, and our response to terrorism—and see how each of these has the potential to be perverted and projected onto China.

China matters because globalization and its benefits to the world are not a given. History allows us to look back and see big assumptions made by the world's best and brightest—the inevitability of peace, the mutual reliance supposedly assured by interconnectivity, the folly of war, the inherent moral advantages of capitalism—and see how they have been proven inadequate time after time. Nothing about our world should be taken for granted, and nothing but death and sorrow awaits an America that chooses trite political blame games when hard choices about our own political economy are needed.

2

The Dragon Slayer's China

"What is missing from the current political and policy calculus is any real sense of urgency about this mission. Instead, we as consumers and corporate executives and government policy makers and voters blithely go about our business as if no storm clouds are on the horizon—much less the prospect of a series of potentially devastating economic, ecological, and military conflicts with, and within, the world's most populous nation."

—Peter Navarro, *The Coming China Wars*

America has traded away its superiority to China. Not just because the United States has lost jobs to China's inexpensive labor—no, because in the pursuit of profit, American businesses willingly looked the other way while China's Communist Party lined its pockets and ensured its future, all at the hands of a naïve American public. The clear moral vision America used to have, the noble ideals of democracy that made it the best country in the world, have been sacrificed at the altar of short-term economic gain. To make matters worse, it is not as if China tried to hide its true face from the world. China's totalitarians and their heavy-handed policies have always been visible to anyone who wanted to see. Or this is what China's most severe critics, the Dragon Slayers camp, would have Americans believe.

Several years ago I struck up a relationship with a Christian pastor in China. We were connected through an outreach program that aimed to establish communication between people in China and the United States.

His letters to me always came through an intermediary and were written out in careful tiny block printing on thin, almost tissue-like paper you could nearly see through. In these letters he educated me about his China. It was a China filled with persecution and fear. Under constant observation by the authorities, this man chose to lead a small group of Christians in a house church under threat of being disbanded or worse.

This was not my China, which is why I needed to understand him and his China. Like many American businessmen, my China presented itself from a comfortable business-class seat in a Boeing 777 that delivered me to either Beijing or Shanghai. There, a servile Chinese porter waited who would whisk me off to my hotel. For the better part of fifteen years, I went back and forth between the United States and China, building several businesses, all the while relishing the experience. My China was full of charm and opportunity; his China was full of menace and oppression. The world needs to understand both if we are to ever grasp the real China.

China is a land of contradictions. A country that embraced cowboy capitalism with all its excesses and luxuries is at the same time a country with egregious human rights violations, restrictions on free speech, and persecution of dissenting political ideas. The temptation is to see only one side of China, usually the side that benefits us the most. For Western businessmen, this can mean ignoring China's problems while emphasizing the country as a potential market and a source for low-priced goods and hoping that the country is in the midst of a major economic and political reform that will ultimately lead it down the path of democracy. But for a growing chorus of Dragon Slayers, voices from Western workers and politicians in particular, their one-sided view of China sees nothing but threats from Beijing on every front: economic, military and political.

Both Dragon Slayers and Panda Huggers see something important and essential about China, but as American politics have grown more dysfunctional, the ability to balance these two contrasting points of view toward China has diminished, and with it our ability to constructively engage Beijing. In the aftermath of the 2008 financial crisis, America and China have greeted each other with increasing mistrust and suspicion. In the heat of the 2012 presidential election, when even the probusiness GOP candidate

Mitt Romney made anti-China rhetoric a part of his stump speech in the Midwest and Rust Belt states, the *New York Times* reported, "two-thirds of Americans now see China as a serious or potential military threat to the United States." The feeling appears to be mutual, as the same survey of Chinese found that "nearly six in ten Chinese believe their country is destined to become the world's leading superpower, and increasing numbers of everyday Chinese believe the United States is trying to prevent them from achieving that status."[1] The 2016 president election made things much, much worse, as both major parties' candidates embraced anti-China and anti-globalization rhetoric as essential parts of their respective campaigns.

The collision course this suggests is as obvious as it may be unavoidable. While once America greeted China from a position of strength, Americans now see China as a threat. And while China once viewed America as the master of the world order, Beijing now believes its own way offers insights and advantages over Western capitalism and democracy. As the rest of the world watches how Beijing and Washington DC navigate today's economic and political challenges, they wonder: is it possible American democratic ideals are not always best? And if they are not, is perhaps authoritarian rule actually preferable to the messy self-government of democracy? Eric Li, a Chinese venture capitalist who lives in Shanghai, is one of the most vocal proponents of the superiority of the Chinese model. In a 2012 *New York Times* op-ed, he wrote, "the West seems incapable of becoming less democratic even when its survival may depend on such a shift. In this sense, America today is similar to the old Soviet Union, which also viewed its political system as the ultimate end. History does not bode well for the American way. Indeed, faith-based ideological hubris may soon drive democracy over the cliff."[2] The rise of fake news, disputes over Russian hacking into the American election, unsubstantiated allegations of voter fraud, all seem to suggest that critics of the American political system have a point.

Today, the Beijing and Washington models of economics and government have squared off against one another: on one side the heavy-handed state determining what is best for its people, and on the other a democracy that elevates the individual's rights above almost all else. These incompatibilities are not new; the tension has always been at play between the two countries. Both in Beijing and Washington DC, loud and increasingly persuasive voices argue for each country to see the other as an enemy. In the United States, the group that sees China as a looming threat to America and the West can be labeled the Dragon Slayers. Their point of view is deeply informed by China's worst side, tellingly revealed when Chinese authorities deny their citizens basic freedoms, or by the saber-rattling that defines too much of China's foreign policy. Dragon Slayers believe the absolute worst things we know about China are also the truest things about China. Because of this, Dragon Slayers believe we should disengage from China and refocus our economic and military plans to address China not as a collaborator, but as a competitor. As evidenced by the 2016 election, Dragon Slayers' day may have finally come, as American economic insecurities have finally created an opening for forces hostile to China and globalization to have more influence.

What gets under the skin of many Dragon Slayers is not only how naïve Americans have been about how trade with China might hurt the American worker, but also how naïve Americans are about China's military ambitions. Aaron Friedberg, a professor at Princeton and a former deputy assistant for national security affairs at the office of the American vice president Dick Cheney, channels this frustration well:

> I [find] myself puzzled and frustrated by what struck me as a willful, blinkered optimism on these matters prevalent at the time in the academic and business communities and across significant portions of the U.S. government. Most of the China experts whom I encountered seem to believe that a Sino-American rivalry was either highly unlikely, too terrifying to contemplate, or (presumably because talking about it might increase the odds that it would occur) too dangerous to discuss. Whatever the reason, *it was not something that serious people spoke about in polite company.*" [emphasis added][3]

That might have been the case five years ago when Friedberg wrote that statement, but as America stands in 2017 at the precipice of the sort of political dysfunction with which it has been unfamiliar since its founding, now is not the time to avoid difficult discussions.

Dragon Slayers have three responsibilities to the American people. First, because Dragon Slayers hold to such a hawkish view of China and because most within this camp argue for the United States to prepare for conflict with China, Dragon Slayers will be advocates of disengagement and war. Whether we agree with their point of view, Dragon Slayers must be held accountable for where their thinking takes America, China, and the world. Second, Dragon Slayers must be required to answer the question of what other option the world had when China first opened to the West. Dragon Slayers point out many of the flaws in how we approached China, but what was the other option? This question plays out today in America's debate around how to engage Cuba and Iran, with one side arguing for disengagement, isolation, sanctions, and even preemptive military strikes, while the other argues for engagement and the cooling-down of what they see as unhelpful rhetoric. Third, Dragon Slayers must provide evidence that China's gain has been because China has not played by the rules, as opposed to China's wins mounting because American domestic policy embraced a type of free market fundamentalism that made helping the American worker all but impossible. These are not trivial differences. Dragon Slayers are anchored on the belief that China's dark side is what most accurately captures the intentions of the government in Beijing and that as such, America should focus most on the country's worst impulses when determining how to engage China.

CHINA'S DARK SIDE

You do not have to look hard to find reasons not to trust China. Setting aside whether China has been good or bad for the American economy in general or the American worker in particular, China's track record on human rights, its lack of political reform, and its heavy-handed use of its military in the region all make the case that Beijing should not be trusted. In the run-up to the 2008 Olympics in Beijing, the Chinese government cracked down on a variety of dissenting political voices.[4] Dragon Slayers were apoplectic both at what happened and at how many westerners looked the other way. To make things even worse, since coming to power in 2013, China's president Xi Jinping has further cracked down on political dissent and actively sought to persecute opposing ideologies, including all manner of restrictions on religious expression.[5] Dragon Slayers pay particular attention to China's dark side and argue that an awareness of this part of China should be the foundation of America's attitudes toward the country and its leaders.

In March 2016 I sat in a conference room behind closed doors at a think tank meeting in Washington DC. I was one of about twenty participants, all experienced China hands and leading experts on United States–China relations. This was a group of heavy hitters, people who knew China well, including a number of Chinese individuals who split their time between the two countries. As our day together unfolded, I had one big insight: a decade ago, this group would have had disagreements at the periphery but more or less a consensus on the core ideas that China's leadership was going to embrace. Any such clarity was now gone. The group was extremely confused and frustrated over how to interpret what Chinese president Xi Jinping was up to. Was he consolidating power so he could push forward on sensitive reforms of the economy? Or was he consolidating power because he saw himself as another Mao, someone who could turn the Chinese presidency into the same sort of near-monarchy that Putin has in Russia? Within our group, no consensus on these questions could be found. That these experts were so divided and unclear as to what was going on in China does little to help well-thought-out policy emerge from the DC beltway. The fact that this was all occurring during a presidential administration at least rhetorically committed to increasing pressure on China is not promising.

However, our uncertainty over China's politics cannot stand in the way of an honest criticism of the country's policies, in particular its human rights violations, which have gotten worse under Xi.[6] This is a problem and a point that Dragon Slayers often return to: after years of looking the other way and choosing to believe that China would gradually get better on human rights, many policy makers have had to acknowledge that the country is going in reverse and ominously so. Of all the points that Dragon Slayers can claim in support of their cynical view of China, the country's backward movement on human rights and use of the state apparatus to pursue dissidents are difficult to deny.

In late June 2016 a Canadian nonprofit released a study showing that China appears still to be involved in active organ harvesting from executed prisoners. As CNN reported, many of the organs appear to have been harvested from "prisoners of conscience locked up for their religious or political beliefs."[7] It is becoming easier to get locked up as a prisoner of conscience in China, not harder. Earlier in the year, Chinese authorities brazenly tracked down domestic dissidents who were safely outside of the country and brought them back to stand trial in China for crimes against the state.[8] Guilty of thought crimes only, these arrested dissidents add to a long list of people imprisoned in China for having the audacity to publicly disagree with the Chinese government.

Across China's prosperous Zhejiang province, after years of relative peace, in 2016 the Chinese government became hostile to Christian churches, chopping down over a thousand church steeples, demolishing a handful of churches, and imprisoning parishioners and pastors who dared protest. One such pastor, Bao Guohua, was convicted and sentenced to fourteen years in prison for resisting Chinese government officials who wanted to remove his church's steeple.[9] One leader of China's underground church movement, where people worship without the Chinese government's official approval, was sentenced in June of 2017 to seven and a half years in prison.[10] Much to the consternation of those who believe China can and should be trusted to ultimately reform and "look more like us," these moves all serve to reinforce the idea that the country cannot be trusted and that its values are fundamentally at odds with ours.

Guy Sorman, an opinion editor at the *Wall Street Journal*, is one such Dragon Slayer. His 2008 book *Empire of Lies* is a classic takedown of those who believe China can ultimately be trusted to reform its political institutions. Sorman forces his readers to answer the question: what are we to make of a country that is willing to arrest, torture, and falsely imprison people whose crime is nothing more than publicly disagreeing with the Chinese government? Sorman's question is not a trivial one, especially when he requires us to wrestle with the motives of those who would argue for a more generous approach toward China: do we look the other way because we really believe their democratization is inevitable so long as we continue a policy of engagement, or do we look away because of personal economic gain?

Former Republican congressman Frank Wolf, who retired in 2015, was one of DC's most infamous Dragon Slayers. He famously shouted down a NASA attempt to collaborate with China in 2011 when he said, "we don't want to give them the opportunity to take advantage of our technology, and we have nothing to gain from dealing with them. And frankly, it boils down to a moral issue.... would you have a bilateral program with Stalin?"[11] When he said this five years ago, plenty of people rolled their eyes, but in the summer of 2016, when Chinese president Xi Jinping's political "reforms" were being called the worst in recent memory, Wolf's rhetoric carries more weight.

It is impossible to factually disagree with Dragon Slayers on this point: China's human rights record is bad. Yet America holds its nose and chooses to do business with any number of governments with similarly bad human rights records. While the reasons for this vary, they are always some combination of economic self-interest and foreign policy. Dragon Slayers hold themselves to a more rigid and disciplined view of these policies and take particular displeasure at the ease with which America has justified its engagement of China on the basis of economic gain. Where advocates of engagement with China see free markets as a way to gradually force the country to change, Dragon Slayers see a long list of myths that do nothing more than ensure the Chinese Communist Party is enriched and empowered and that its future stranglehold on the Chinese people is ensured.

Not all Dragon Slayers are alike. Dragon Slayers exist along a spectrum that ranges from those like Peter Navarro, the author and documentarian of *Death by China*, an assistant to President Trump as the director of trade and industrial policy, and director of the White House National Trade Council, who believes China is America's enemy and that our policies should reflect this, to those who begrudgingly acknowledge that a limited policy of engagement is better than outright hostilities. Page one, paragraph one of Navarro's book *Death by China* begins this way: "Death by China. This is the very real risk we all now face as the world's most populous nation and soon-to-be largest economy is rapidly turning into the planet's most efficient assassin."[12] Not every Dragon Slayer believes China is a military threat to the United States, just as not every Dragon Slayer believes China's role in globalization has savaged the American worker. What unifies Dragon Slayers is the assertion that America has been naïve in our approach to China. To many Dragon Slayers, mixed motives have led American businesses and politicians to look past China's dark side and to believe the myths they assert drove globalization's advance.

DRAGON SLAYERS AND GLOBALIZATION

To many Americans, China as an exciting potential market is a new idea, but it should not be. It might be a surprise for many to know that in the 1930s American businesses rushed into China to chase the exact same things being pursued now: new markets, untapped consumer demand, and a rising middle class. Carl Crow, a famous old China hand living in Shanghai during the thirties, wrote a series of business books designed to get American business executives thrilled about the potential of selling into China's growing middle class. Crow's most famous book, *400 Million Customers*, was an attempt to pull the covers back on the China market and what he saw as the untold riches available there.

During this same period, *Life* magazine photographer Jack Birns captured a version of China that anyone who has traveled there recently will recognize. His pictures show the Shanghai of the thirties as a hustling and bustling city of commerce. In one of Birns's photos, stretched over a bustling street in Shanghai is a large billboard of Hollywood starlet Lana Turner, hawking soap. Another rooftop billboard shows a provocatively dressed American woman advertising cigarettes. In their day, these were signs of globalization, of the near certainty American and European companies had that China would become a great export market.

What Birns did not know was that China was on the cusp of a violent revolution. His camera lens soon stopped capturing the casual moments of vibrant city life and began to record moments of brutality and death.

In one of his more infamous pictures he shows a beheaded insurgent captured and killed near the Songjiang district in Shanghai. After the beheading the rebel's head was rammed onto a steel pike jutting out of a nearby retaining wall. Dragon Slayers have not forgotten that the China who played host to Lana Turner and other voluptuous and swimsuit-clad American gals can quickly collapse and that something darker lies beneath all of the money to be made in China. For Dragon Slayers, the brutality of these moments from China's history says something essential that cannot be forgotten: this country is capable of extreme violence and is more fragile than most will acknowledge.

Dragon Slayers are suspicious about the economic motives that lead many Western businessmen in particular to embrace China. Several years ago I had the opportunity to dine with a successful businessman who owned several factories in China. This man prided himself on being a staunch conservative who used his personal fleet of jets to ferry around Republican presidential candidates during the GOP primary, something that provided him an opportunity to question them one-on-one about their policies. Over dinner, he loudly proclaimed about how easy it was to do business in China and how the local leaders would do almost anything he asked in order to get him to expand his factories. After listening to him talk about one particular situation in which a plot of land had been razed to the ground for one of his factories, I asked him, "but what about the conservative principles behind eminent domain? Does it bother you at all that the government simply took those people's land without any due process?" For a moment, his chair seemed to swallow him up, until he leaned forward and said emphatically, "Maybe. But it's good for me and my businesses."

What Dragon Slayers see here is a hypocrisy that puts profit above all else: above workers, above political principle, above your own country's needs. This man considered himself a patriot and a proud American. Yet as long as he stood to benefit personally, his political principles were secondary. I suspect the first time China does him wrong, he will turn into one of the most virulent and bellicose critics of China. But for now he presses on and looks the other way at actions that, if they took place here in the United States, would have him screaming of treason. Dragon Slayers fear China has unwittingly figured out something essential about capitalism: that in its pursuit to maximize profits, it will happily hollow itself out and trade away most of its advantages, so long as the smallest potential for profit can be found. A small group of Dragon Slayers believe China's leaders have always known this about foreigners and point toward several thousand years of history in which China falls behind the technology or standard of living from the West, gradually opens to Western influence, then shuts when westerners start to push on what they believe to be necessary reforms to China's politics.

You do not have to convince me that the economic justification that promotes globalization, and China's part in it specifically, can be decidedly mixed. Nearly a decade ago I was in China sourcing parts for a product that would end up in several of America's big box retailers. I will never forget walking through one factory in particular where a young woman was methodically working away on a loud machine press while her infant laid next to her, nestled in a pile of dirty shop rags. Grandiose narratives about the good of globalization for China's rural poor seemed small and vain in that moment, and yet for all of the Dragon Slayers' principled resistance, it is difficult to wonder where China would be without a policy of engagement and free trade. Dragon Slayers hone in on a different and equally provocative point: the combined force of these myths and the distorted priorities that emphasize personal economic gain have not only clouded our judgment about China, they have also proven that personal liberty *can be* severed from economic freedom.

FREE MARKETS ≠ FREE PEOPLE

The possibility that free markets do not lead to free people upends nearly thirty years of America's policies toward China and has also provoked leaders in the United States and western Europe to wonder whether China's way of governing might be better than theirs. Reflecting on the Greek government's pursuit of what amounted to an emergency loan from China, Nathan Gardels channeled this very concern: "In a consumer democracy, where the feedback signals from politics, the media, and the market all steer society toward immediate self-gratification, there is scarce political capacity for the kind of long-term thinking, planning, and continuity of governance which has so far been responsible for China's rise. When scarce political capacity and consumer democracy are joined with robust technological prowess, both the societal and generational impacts are amplified and extended well beyond the present moment and local environment."[13] What Gardels is poking at is the idea that freedom may not be either the ultimate good or the best form of government at particular moments in time.

Dragon Slayers channel this misgiving in a more focused way: they hold to a core belief that free markets do not always lead to free people. To their way of thinking, authoritarian countries can remain as such, choosing only to open their economies enough to reap the economic rewards of having an open society without ever fully addressing ongoing repression of free speech and political dissent or encouraging new political parties to form and vie for power. A more nuanced point of view, which a handful of Dragon Slayers attempt to argue, is that China never really had free markets in the first place. As such, outsiders' hope that people in China would be free in the same sense we are in the West was always naïve. For countries across Southeast Asia, the Middle East, Africa, and even parts of Latin America, what has become known as the Beijing Model, or as some have termed it, the Beijing Consensus, has come into vogue. The Beijing Consensus presents the world with this idea: authoritarian governments are not inherently bad—in fact for some societies they are necessary—nor are they incompatible with free market reforms. When contrasted with American values, this is not a trivial disagreement.

The United States was founded on the idea that individual liberty is essential, and that any government involvement should be limited to what is necessary to protect the rights of the individual. Americans believe that government exists to support the individual's rights to worship, speak freely, and act within the established boundaries society has established. Borne of the European Enlightenment, these ideals are central not only to our belief about the role and shape of government, but they have also informed the relationship between our government and our economy. In particular, per these ideals, an effective economy requires a minimal role for government and a maximized role for the individual. Our view of freedom is not divisible: a person is not truly free if he can trade but cannot speak freely, worship where he wishes, or move unencumbered within his country. The link between economic and personal liberty is, for Americans, fundamental and inseverable. In China this link does not exist. In fact the Communist Party, to the point of persecuting those who assert these individual rights, actively denies such a connection.

Dragon Slayers acknowledge that China's leaders are motivated by fear of the mob, a concern that China's history over the last century supports. However, Dragon Slayers also believe that these fears are overblown and that they are nothing more than excuses for the party to resist reforms that would gradually disempower them and give the Chinese people more say in the country's political process. Both sides of this debate recognize that Beijing's political class is suspicious as to whether they can trust the individual Chinese with political freedom. America has been, in the best and truest sense of the word, a laboratory of ideas Europeans developed and fought over during the Enlightenment. The net result of the two different paths is that America trusts the individual and views the government with suspicion, while China trusts the government and views the individual with suspicion.

As a consequence of Beijing's mistrust of its own people, the country's leaders believe the way forward for China will require a strong—even authoritarian—government to establish limitations designed to maintain order. Dragon Slayers believe these limitations will engender the very sort of strife and turmoil China's leaders hope to avoid: China would be better off relaxing its stranglehold on freedom to dissent, worship, and participation in government. Losing control, as many critics of China have pointed out, could well mean not only the country's spinning out of control but also the death of many of the corrupt leaders hiding inside the Chinese Communist Party's ranks. This sheds some light on why the Beijing Consensus is of interest to so many autocrats and totalitarians around the world: the leadership in countries like Iran faces similar pressures.

Despots and authoritarians around the world know that whatever other claims to legitimacy they may have, it is difficult to stay in power if the economy crumbles. This lesson was powerfully made during the Arab Spring, when long-standing grievances over political repression, the lack of economic opportunities, and fears over inflation spilled over and engulfed the region, violently throwing rulers from power. Whatever their political ideologies, most dictators in the Middle East knew economic or political reform would likely result in their deaths and the destruction of the fortunes they had hoarded away over years of skimming from government programs. The plight of Hosni Mubarak's family in Egypt after he fell is only one example of this fear being realized.[14] So what are leaders in similar positions in other countries supposed to do? The advent of the Beijing Consensus entirely changed their calculus. Now the mullahs in Iran might have found a way to stay in control and still tap into opportunities the free market provided. In between these two extremes are Asian countries, most notably Singapore, Taiwan, and South Korea, whose political systems come up well short of the American ideal, yet manage to provide more freedoms to their citizens than does China.

The Beijing Model was a counterpoint to the American one: a country could have an authoritarian government, participate in the global free market, and manage to stay in power, all while addressing the peoples' need for economic growth. To leaders of totalitarian systems, the fundamental insight from the Beijing Consensus was that poor people would trade political freedom for economic growth. This was earth-shattering. The American model said democracy was a precondition for economic growth; since democracy was not something these autocrats and totalitarians believed in, their economic models were stuck. The Beijing Model changed all of this by showing that free markets did not always have to lead to free people. In this way, China's approach presented the world with the possibility that capitalism may have resurrected Communism.

HAS CAPITALISM RESURRECTED COMMUNISM?

Dragon Slayers make a troubling point about why China has opened to the West: because it would make China's leaders rich and ultimately let them stay in control. To Dragon Slayers, China opened because it saw a path forward to ensure the viability of the Communist Party, not because reformers wanted to see China liberalize. Just enough economic engagement would allow the Communist Party to stay in control. But this is very much a case of Monday-morning quarterbacking. It was by no means clear, in the period after Mao Zedong and Richard Nixon first met, that normalization would peacefully progress or that China would manage to pull itself up from a half century of decline. No, the China of the 1970s and 1980s was weak, beset by any number of political problems and economic setbacks. In order to understand what was happening when the United States and China first engaged, it is helpful to flash back to when China decided to let American economics and politics begin to gain influence within its borders.

When Mao first pivoted toward the United States in 1972, he found a country eager to receive his friendship. For the United States, Mao's interest was the penultimate Cold War victory. Ultimate victory over Communism was still a decade away, but Mao's decision was a major step toward America's final Cold War victory over the Soviet Union. The original policy formulation from the United States toward China was simple: engage China, and China will disengage from the Soviet Union. Coupled with this was a subcurrent of thinking that proved incredibly powerful then and remains equally so: engage China, and China will become more like us. This idea created the policy framework that brought the two countries together then and that continues to knit us together now.

An economic justification (China as a market to sell into), together with a political one (China would democratize if we would only engage them politically), was tied to the belief that China presented the United States with a critical strategic buffer against the Soviet Union. Together, these three components—the economic and political justifications and foreign policy—would function with amazing symmetry and continuity through three decades of American presidents. Even in the darkest of hours, as questions from Dragon Slayers about China's ugly authoritarian impulses in the wake of the Tiananmen Square atrocities became unavoidable, American insistence that China would ultimately prove to be a good and trustworthy partner owed its support to these three factors. Dragon Slayers believe that from the late nineties up to today, our approach to

China has been too deeply wedded to a framework that was borne in the throes of the Cold War and that must be updated to reflect the world today.

In the aftermath of the Soviet Union's collapse, America had the opportunity to reposition its policies toward China. However, our hands were full given what was going on in Europe and the former Soviet Union. Once the smoke cleared in Moscow and America could look more clearly into the inner workings of the Soviet empire, it became increasingly clear that while everyone might wish for China to magically become a democracy, that was unlikely and might not even be desirable. The idea that China's system might implode while the Soviet Union was also collapsing was disconcerting not just to China but to the United States as well.

China also watched the Soviet Union fall apart and made note of the fact that political reforms that moved too quickly could get out of hand. This still constitutes much of how China's leadership views political reform: too many reforms undertaken too quickly will lead to instability, which is bad for the party, the country, and (they believe) the people. Perhaps just as important, the belief within most of Washington that the world cannot afford to see China destabilize guided and still guides much of the West's policy toward Beijing.

Across the defunct Iron Curtain, once-stable Soviet satellite states went through their own revolutions. Americans, for the most part, applauded: the long-awaited victory over the evil of Communism was taking place. While those in the West found these moments to celebrate, China's leadership found them reason for fear. Former George H. W. Bush administration national security advisor Brent Scowcroft wrote with Bush in their book *A World Transformed* about their sense of what China's leadership was thinking as the Iron Curtain fell: "When [Romanian strongman] Ceausescu was toppled, I believe the Chinese leaders panicked. It had appeared to me that they had taken great comfort from his apparent impregnability."[15]

Washington and Beijing were asking the same question: would China be next? While the easy answer from the point of view of American democracy was "hopefully, yes," the more practical realization by those in Washington was that China's transition to a more liberal form of government would need to be more ordered than the former Soviet Union's. Given China's not-too-distant revolutionary past and civil war, it would be in everyone's best interest if the transition were quiet and orderly. Russia's disordered chaos as well as the depth of poverty and dysfunction that surrounded the Soviet Union's former client states after the Soviet collapse instructed American policy makers. While the United States wanted China to become a democracy, Washington also wanted the process to be gradual and coherent, not violent and disjointed.

The hope that China would ultimately—if gradually—form a democratic government has proven to be one of the most potent justifications for our policy of engagement. It has been used to support maintaining our relationship with Beijing post-Tiananmen, as well as during key battles over trade policy such China's ascent to the World Trade Organization and its classification as a most favored nation. During the battle over the latter, President Clinton referenced the hope for a democratic China as part of why it was important to extend most favored nation status. Clinton believed intertwining our two economies "offers us the best opportunity to lay the basis for long-term sustainable progress on human rights and for the advancement of our other interests with China."[16] Those "other interests" President Clinton referred to? Democracy and freedom. America's relative political and economic strength then led to broad support for those who wanted to trust China, while Dragon Slayers threw up their hands in frustration at what they thought was a naïve belief that China's Communist Party would ever democratize.

Clinton and President Bush before him believed China would make economic reforms that would breathe life not only into the free market but also into the forces of democracy. In the midst of what many saw as a historical high in American power not seen since the days immediately after World War II, allowing this policy the space to be proven seemed fairly low risk. What few foresaw is that as China grew, it walked a frustrating line between free markets and restrictions on individual freedoms. As China's ability to do this continued, Dragon Slayers began to wonder if China's success was pointing other authoritarian systems toward the idea that economic and political freedoms were in fact fully separable.

With China's success has come a chorus of voices from the Dragon

Slayers' camp, including such people as James Mann who believe that Americans have fundamentally misread the intention of China's leaders. Mann argues that China has no intention to democratize. He wants Americans to ask themselves whether we are going to be pleased to have enriched and empowered a Communist Party that has no intention of ever giving its people the freedoms we take for granted. As he puts it, "What if, in twenty-five or thirty years from now, a wealthier, more powerful China continues to be run by a one-party regime that still represses organized political dissent much as it does today, while at the same time China is also open to the outside world and, indeed is deeply intertwined with the rest of the world through trade, investment, and other economic ties?"[17] Or, as Dragon Slayers might put it more simply: what if capitalism has resurrected Communism?

3

The Panda Hugger's China

"Most Chinese scholars harbor the hope that China will 'surpass' traditional forms of democracy as practiced in the rest of the world—especially the imagined 'Western model'—and introduce to the world a new system that will be 'even better.' . . . As one Western scholar notes: 'It remains possible that some day the Asian, perhaps even the Chinese, vision of the best form of government will become the dominant vision.' If so, it would be a cause for celebration because everyone benefits when a more just system is available."
—Bruce Gilley, *China's Democratic Future*

Entertain with me a future based on a different path from what the United States and China actually took, a path that would have seen China follow in the footsteps of the fallen Soviet Union and neurotic North Korea. Imagine with me that the year is 2020. China's new president, Liu Mingfu, has addressed the Chinese people in his first public television appearance since the dissolution of the country's Standing Committee. Some outsiders are calling Liu's ascent a coup, plain and simple. The reasons are not hard to understand: since the collapse of the Soviet Union in December of 1991, China has lurched forward, trying to bully its neighbors and intentionally destabilize the world order in the hopes it might gain some small advantage over the Western political and economic system China's leaders fear.

Since the Soviet Union ceased to be, China believed its destiny was to take Mao's version of Communism, a marked improvement over the original formulation by Marx and Lenin, and spread it around the world. As China watched the former Soviet Union spiral out of control, with the state's natural resources and manufacturing assets stolen from under the government's nose, Beijing pressed forward with the belief that it now was the vanguard in the struggle for Communist principles.

But China has not been able to live up to this, and the political recriminations that have led a hard-liner like Liu to take power now appear ready to push the world into war. The collapse of the Soviet Union created an opportunity for China to be perceived as a great power, but Beijing was not ready. Politically, in the aftermath of Mao's death, the country had rallied under the leadership of Deng Xiaoping for a little while until hard-liners committed to Mao's near-god-like status recognized that Deng's reforms were going to push China away from Mao's revered Communist vision toward a more liberal economic and political system. For the third time in his life, Deng found himself sent back to a reeducation camp, this time never to emerge. Rather than reforming its struggling economy, China had doubled down on Mao's axioms, diverting more and more of its political and economic capital toward ill-fated modernization programs.

From the outside looking in, China's problems were obvious. Always a country that had struggled to feed itself, with a long history of destabilizing food shortages, China had experienced its second massive famine in the modern era with deaths peaking in late 1997. Estimates vary widely given the sensitive nature of this information, but based on the amount of foreign aid China blackmailed the world into providing, up to 191 million people may have starved to death.

Speaking of blackmail, China turned the Soviet Union's sclerotic approach with the West into an art form. China became the dysfunctional second cousin to the Soviet Union: more people, blunter policies, clumsier interactions with the West, all coupled to a unique ability to do precisely the wrong thing at the absolute worst moment. China also perfected the art of knowing who inside of China to keep rich, who to keep poor, and who to simply disappear. The country was always opaque to the West, but now it had become what some people called the Hermit Kingdom. It was almost as if the economic successes of China's regional peers, countries like Japan and the reunified Korea in particular, made Beijing want to withdraw even further into its own world.

In 1996 China's saber-rattling in the Straits of Formosa (the narrow strip of sea that separates the Chinese mainland from Taiwan), escalated to actual exchange of hostilities, as China's initial missiles volley toward military bases on Taiwan's western shores resulted in a response by Taiwan. Only the United States' heavy-handed intervention in the form of two nuclear-powered carrier battle groups steamed into the conflict zone prevented this from escalating into war. The most prominent China hawk that vocally pushed for an even more aggressive response by the Chinese military was the People's Liberation Army (PLA) colonel Liu Mingfu. By the mid-2000s, Liu had seen his point of view embraced by the Chinese public. He had successfully convinced the Chinese government and its people that the United States was a mortal danger to China's security. In achieving this, Liu had been embraced by a China hungry to see the country take its rightful place as a great power. Since then, his gradual accumulation of power had resulted in his becoming China's unquestioned leader.

Liu addressed a nation that could only be described as schizophrenic. Years of indoctrination had resulted in people who could not think for themselves. They took whatever the Dear Leader said on TV or radio as gospel. This had resulted in a perverse pride that China was in some way special and that to the extent the Chinese people had known suffering, it was all for the greater good. Fears of political recrimination had completely suppressed any dissenting voices who found this thinking ridiculous. Reeducation camps had gone from being a rite of passage to a place people simply disappeared into, with a death notice from the camp as evidence the Chinese state had swallowed up yet another life. In his first televised speech since the so-called coup, Liu made his thinking absolutely clear:

> For China's military rise, there should be a powerful military force able to effectively maintain and achieve national unity, and control and crack down on separatist forces. It must be an effective force in the Taiwan Strait to counter U.S. military intervention, which would deter the United States from supporting Taiwanese independence with

force. The goal of China's military rise is to make the United States unable to afford to contain China. With this military rise, China will be able to prosper without being peacefully contained by the U.S., and will also be able to contain the U.S. China's military strength has to be more powerful than any rivals in the world to the degree and level that no nation can contain China's rise. No country shall set a ceiling for China's power.[1]

THE CHINA THAT COULD HAVE BEEN

Can you tell which of the above actually happened, and which is fiction? Liu Mingfu is an actual retired senior colonel from the PLA. His book, *The China Dream*, from which the earlier quote is taken, was published in 2010 and stands as a clarion call to China hawks to arm themselves so they can project Chinese power across the region and the world. He is far from being the most radical voice currently shaping Chinese policy. There are a large number of Chinese who reveled in Donald Trump's election because they believe he marks the demise of American power. Reflecting on why, in general, so many Chinese Americans in particular supported Trump's candidacy, Kaiser Kuo wrote at *SupChina*, "a distressingly high number understand that a Trump victory would take the wind out of America's sanctimonious sails when it comes to pushing liberal democracy and would cherish just such an outcome."[2] Many Chinese forcefully assert that the next era belongs to an ascendant China, one able to bend America to its wishes in the same way they believe America has done to China. What is also not fiction is that China has a history of massive food shortages, including the most severe famine in history, when approximately 36 million Chinese starved to death between 1958 and 1962.[3] And the Taiwan Strait Crisis did happen in 1996, with the U.S. Navy having to intervene in order to prevent a regional war.[4]

Where I have taken liberty is in my description of a China that turned inwards after the collapse of the Soviet Union. Specifically, I have knit together a narrative that takes the path North Korea took and ask what our world would look like if China had become a much bigger version of the troubles we see nearly every week from Pyongyang. What would our world look like if, instead of a famine in North Korea that killed somewhere around 3.5 million people in 2007, a similar famine had struck China and taken the lives of the same percentage of Chinese as it did North Koreans? Do we really think the death of up to 191 million Chinese, on the heels of their terrible famine of 1958–62, would not have spilled out from China's borders, destabilizing the world in ways that make the Syrian refugee crisis pale in comparison? If China acted the way North Korea does now, would China be using its nuclear arsenal to threaten and cajole the world into getting what it wanted? In 1957 Mao infamously shrugged off his fear of how his country would fare in a nuclear war: "I'm not afraid of nuclear war. There are 2.7 billion people in the world; it doesn't matter if some are killed. China has a population of 600 million; even if half of them are killed, there are still 300 million people left. I'm not afraid of anyone."[5] It is hard to believe China's approach to being poor and isolated would not have made our current predicament with North Korea seem trivial in comparison.

The group called "Panda Huggers" chooses to see what is good about China. They believe that America should continue along the path of constructive engagement with China. In particular, they believe China could have easily taken another path that looked more like the one North Korea has taken, one that would have led to extreme pain and suffering in China and potentially around the world. To Panda Huggers, China's progress since Deng's reforms in the 1980s shows a country more dedicated to market reforms and political liberalization than not. Yes, nearly every Panda Hugger is frustrated with the "two steps forward, one step back" that seem to characterize contemporary Chinese politics. But at the end of the day, Panda Huggers believe that free markets go hand-in-hand with free people. To them it is only a matter of time before China realizes it cannot liberalize its economy and stir up ideas about individualism, innovation, and entrepreneurship without also laying the foundation for some sort of democratic government. To Panda Huggers, while this process may take longer than originally thought, the outcome is inevitable: a freer, more stable China that looks more like the West than something Mao would have recognized.

Panda Huggers offer a compelling counterargument: do we really want to live in a world in which China did not open to the West? "Fine," say Panda

Huggers, "we didn't get everything right when it comes to our China policy. But what really is the alternative?" In today's political climate, where tearing down the status quo has become the defining political agenda animating civic discourse, have we lost the ability to recognize that while we might have got some things wrong about China, overall the world is better off for not having to watch China implode in the immediate aftermath of the Soviet Union's collapse? It is critical to acknowledge that both points of view exist on a spectrum: not every Dragon Slayer wants to go to war with China tomorrow, and not every Panda Hugger wants the West to forever view China as a perpetual teenager, close to adulthood but still in need of parental guidance.

Panda Huggers once enjoyed the upper hand. They successfully argued that bringing China into the global order would result in a more stable world. In a *Foreign Policy* podcast after the 2016 election, David Rothkopf, a former senior member of the Clinton administration who handled trade negotiations, reflected in a defeated tone on what the election said about how Democrats had lost touch with their traditional political constituents, "listen, I was one of those who went out and sold the idea to the American public that a rising tide would lift all boats, and I was wrong."[6] Globalization became synonymous with American values, in particular as both conservatives and liberals agreed that free markets would inevitably lead to free people. But Panda Huggers may have overextended themselves. China's entry into the global economy destabilized a specific group of blue-collar workers in America who no longer felt globalization was going to create opportunities for them. Globalization and the unrelenting pressure of purely financial investors who had no particular commitment to those workers, their companies, or their communities made many Americans feel unsafe and insecure. At the same time, their traditional political advocates in the Democratic Party stopped believing that politics could play a meaningful role ensuring equal opportunity for all. Instead, across Middle America, people came to believe globalization was the poster child for how elites in both parties had sold out the American worker to line their own pockets. Donald Trump the person may not have been predictable; Donald Trump the phenomena should have been.

When hardworking blue-collar workers come to believe they have been sold a bill of goods by the establishment, they will look for someone—anyone—who is willing to be their personal wrecking ball. In times of plenty and relative security, Panda Huggers could push back against all of this, but that has now changed, and with it the ability to prevent conflict between the United States and China has decreased.

Yet these criticisms come up well short of fully delegitimizing Panda Huggers' views on China. In fact, America could very well have normalized relations with China just as it did without the negative impact to American workers, if only Washington had not descended into partisan quarreling and stopped working toward solutions that meaningfully benefit the American middle class. Panda Huggers may prove to have been entirely right about China, while sharing equal blame with Dragon Slayers in their mutual lack of attention to America's political and economic needs. Where Dragon Slayers paint Panda Huggers as naïve, the latter group responds with important context specific to where China is coming from: namely, the idea that an impoverished, isolated, and insecure country the size of China has no other way to enter the modern era than how it did.

Panda Huggers bristle at the idea that their approach to China has been naïve. Most argue not only that their approach is more realistic and pragmatic than that offered by Dragon Slayers but also that the latter's approach to China inevitably leads to war. Overall, Panda Huggers emphasize the context of where China has come from: by the late 1970s, China was an industrial wasteland, a country without a manufacturing base, a viable economy of any sort, and no ability to compete globally. China was hungry, politically vulnerable, and shamed by an ideology that had consumed the very fabric of their culture. While today this idea of China as an emasculated country seems far-fetched, it holds particular truths that Panda Huggers believe about China and, even more importantly, that China believes about itself.

Four factors influence Panda Huggers' view of China. First, China's century of humiliation at the hands of Western powers meant the West needed to grant China some special latitudes in terms of its development. Second, China's emergence from a fractured feudal and agrarian state was always going to require some sort of authoritarianism as part of a transition into a more mature and democratic form of government. Third, the sheer size differences between America and China would unavoidably magnify whatever problems already existed in Western industrial policy. Fourth, China's current economic modernization is trying to pull off in fifty years what it took America nearly two hundred to achieve.

A CENTURY OF HUMILIATION

Where America's civil war propelled it forward into a positive future, China's civil war was the final straw in a hundred-year period the Chinese reference as their "century of humiliation" or "century of shame." China's century of humiliation began with the First Opium War in 1839, when Britain and the Qing dynasty went to war. It may seem far-fetched today, but this war boiled down to the Chinese government's desire to keep Britain from selling opium to its people. Sales of opium had created approximately 2 million addicts across the country and had led to all manner of societal problems. One woodcut from the era shows a Chinese man, addled and drug dependent, dragging his wife by the hair in the hopes he can sell her into slavery and receive enough money to continue purchasing opium. Britain's role in the opium trade reflected one of the darkest sides of colonialism: the view that the Chinese were an acceptable people upon which to unleash the evil of opium in pursuit of profit. Until the modern era, China had not really recovered from the Opium Wars. Today, many Chinese draw a straight line from the Opium Wars to the Chinese Civil War and the belief that China should be given leeway to modernize its economy given its poor treatment by foreign powers for much of the last century.

While America emerged from its civil war united and economically empowered, China's civil war led to Communism, famine, and a ravaged industrial base. Until the end of World War II, China's most critical ports were carved into pieces for other great powers to use as they wished. At the end of America's civil war, the country could stand confident and comfortable that its borders were secure and that it had no fear of another regional power. China had no such confidence. One of the most important differences between how America and China developed in the modern era is the legacy of severe conflict with our respective neighbors. America had a history of conflicts with the United Kingdom, but the Atlantic Ocean provided an important barrier of protection. China's close proximity to countries that in its recent past have meant it harm, such as Japan and Russia, is much more problematic.

Americans rightfully understand the Revolutionary War as our nation's defining conflict. That war embodies our views of individual independence, the role of government, even the usefulness of political violence at particular moments in time. Because it serves as a specific event against which we can measure our nation's birth, it is easy to overlook the larger picture of what was happening globally as we fought for our independence. The European continental powers were jockeying for preeminence, setting in motion rivalries that can be traced to both world wars. Monarchies were transitioning into modern nation-states, seeking to expand their territories through annexation or war. From 1700 to 1800, Europe experienced almost two dozen wars as continental powers struggled to establish order.[7]

Beyond these conflicts, internal revolutions during this period over the rightful role of the state and religious institutions sent powerful earthquakes around the world. As European empires pursued global expansion, they laid claims on colonies from Africa to North America to Asia. Both China and the United States served as proxies for larger conflicts between European powers. France's support of the American colonialists was motivated in part by the French desire to see British power take a hit. Interestingly enough, both the United States and China would find British cannons pointed at them during this period. That the United States beat back the British threat while the Chinese succumbed to foreign powers remains a source of major insecurity in China, and one Panda Huggers recognize should be taken into account when creating policy toward China.

British and American tensions did not easily resolve themselves; in fact, the two went to war again in 1812, as the United States sought to push the British out of what would become Ontario. The United States' military outing on this occasion ended with little in the way of new territory. Much more successful were the relatively peaceful westward expansions fueled by the Louisiana Purchase in 1803, coupled with the westward immigration it set in motion. In 1845 the United States found itself at war with Mexico over the Republic of Texas as the state entered the Union. The once-nascent sense of space and place that had initially pushed the American colonists into Canada had, by the end of the Mexican-American War of 1845, evolved into a much stronger and well-defined idea known as Manifest Destiny, the claim that America had the right and obligation to settle the continental west.

Panda Huggers recognize that as any emerging power begins to assert itself, it first carves out its place regionally, then seeks to find its way globally. What China is doing now in the South China Sea, Africa, and South America is what every rising power has done before it in both form and function. Panda Huggers view this as a reality that cannot be resisted and go so far as to say that an attempt to arrest a rising power is one of the most common causes of regional and global war. The American idea of Manifest Destiny created much of what still constitutes the United States' perspective on its historical uniqueness and the country's obligation to export its ideals. This remains a powerful part of America's self-conception and its responsibility to stand as a vanguard against those who threaten democracy and freedom. At its best, this has led us to stand strong against Communism; at its worst, it has made it too easy for foreign policy misadventures, most recently in Iraq. China will not be without its own version of Manifest Destiny, and Panda Huggers believe this is a foundational truth that should be recognized.

In contrast to America's regional development, China's history has been marked by domination by various great powers: Europe (Britain specifically), Japan, and Russia. In each of these cases, China seemed destined to play the role of pawn as the other more "important" chess pieces attempted to strategize their way to global domination. European powers viewed China as a potential market for both their legitimate (textiles) and illegitimate (opium) goods. Contests over market access played an important role in driving the Qing dynasty out of power and led to China's most important port cities coming under the governance of European powers.

Eager to follow in the footsteps of the great European powers that Japan saw colonizing large swaths of Asia, Japan took the Meiji Era (1868–1912) to build its industrial base and pursue its own territorial expansion. In many ways, China was the first victim. Focused on the Korean peninsula, the First Sino-Japanese War (1894–95) saw Japan wipe out much of the Chinese fleet at the Battle of the Yalu River. As part of the agreement the European powers would broker, the Chinese ceded Taiwan to the Japanese Empire. The Second Sino-Japanese War took place against the backdrop of World War II, as Japan looked into China for a source of land and raw materials. The conflict between 1931 and the end of the Pacific campaign in 1945 spoke for more casualties than any other theater.

After World War II, China's relations with the European continent could have settled down, but China found itself in regional competition with the Soviet Union and India. As Mao settled into power, the relationship between China and the Soviet Union was a source of constant tension. Even though the two countries both claimed to be adherents to Marx, on practical matters the two struggled to agree. Aaron Friedberg, writing in his book *A Contest for Supremacy: China, America, and the Struggle for Mastery in Asia*, notes that "the personality clashes, strategic debates, and ideological disagreements that had roiled Sino-Soviet relations since the death of Stalin had blossomed by the 1960s into an open, undisguised animosity bordering on mutual hatred."[8] This underlying conflict between the two countries occasionally sparked up, as it did in 1969 over a border disagreement. Ultimately the tension between the Chinese and Soviets would get bad enough that it afforded an opening for Nixon's diplomacy.

Between the early 1960s and the late 1980s, Sino-Indian relations gradually deteriorated, with the two countries finding themselves in armed conflict on three different occasions. The first was in 1962 over a border in the Himalayas and disputed territorial claims of an area roughly the size of Switzerland that was shared between China and India; however, as with most geopolitical conflicts, this clash had other causes. The two other factors that played a role were the granting of asylum by Indian officials to the exiled Dalai Lama and a split within the Indian Communist Party. Fought to a relative standstill, the conflict sparked up again in 1967 and once more some twenty years later over many of the same territorial disputes. In August 2017 video surfaced of Chinese and Indian army forces skirmishing—thankfully only with fists and thrown stones—in the Himalayan region the two countries had previously gone to war over.[9]

Overall, this serves as a foundational point for Panda Huggers: China's last century has been characterized by a series of conflicts that have not gone China's way. Over and over China has struggled to defend itself from outside threats and has been left in a weakened state that allowed internal strife to further distress the country's economic and political systems. Panda Huggers recognize China's insecurities and suggest that the interpretation of China must take into account the very real wrongs that have been done against it in the modern era. Nowhere is this to suggest that Panda Huggers argue for anyone to ignore to China's misdeeds; rather, they argue China has to be seen as a particular type of rising power that has real security concerns based on recent history.

RULE BY BENEVOLENT DICTATORS

No greater difference exists between American and China than in how both countries have developed politically. Of the differences in how our two countries evolved, Panda Huggers believe four are most important: the development of a rule of law, the aftermath of feudalism in China, the role of representative government, and the timing of the two countries' civil wars. The common thread connecting each of these four differences is the realization that America's political development embodied the insights and ideals that came from the Enlightenment: ideas that went to the heart of how our government was conceived, implemented, and held accountable by the people. The lineage of China's political development is much more fragile and fragmented, a realization Panda Huggers believe should help us understand what we can—and cannot—expect as China modernizes.

Early American life was predominantly agrarian. Important to America's agricultural dominance was its emphasis on the role and right of the individual to subjugate the land to his use with minimal taxation. During this same period, when China could have embraced much of the West's formula (mechanized agriculture and transportation in particular), the country was bound to what was essentially a feudal system. Just as European feudal lords had done, Chinese feudal lords viewed individuals as property, as part and parcel of the feudal lord's holdings. In the United States, the rule of law was one of our earliest values. While in certain parts of the lawless American West this ideal took time to take hold, it was an immediate fixture of the American colonies. Conversely, the Chinese system of law did not take a similar sense of justice purely from an established book of rules, regulations, and responsibilities but rather from the word of a ruler. This may in part explain why the cult of Mao could take such a hold on China; he was, in many ways, simply a Communist version of the thousand-year-old tradition of an all-knowing Chinese emperor. As such, his mandates were unquestionable.

China's view of representative government also reflects lessons derived from the legacy of Confucianism. An integral part of Confucianism is the role of hierarchy and obedience to rulers, in particular the wise Mandarins whose job it was to rule over the people as stewards who carefully weighed policies only as a benevolent technocrats could. The ideal Confucian ruler was someone who would educate himself and seek to pursue policies designed to better the lives of the average person. Because it was his job to be the perfect leader, the people could trust him fully. This same dynamic would be played out through millennia within Chinese families, where the father was not to be questioned. The net effect of this has been to instill deeply in China's culture the need to go along, not rock the boat, and trust that their leaders know best. This helped to create a climate where leaders such as Mao could come to power, rule disastrously, and remain confident they could hold onto power.

How different could America be from China in this regard? Almost every part of the founding myths of the United States has to do with rugged individualism and the need for representative government. The first colonists were escaping the oppression of the English monarchy; the Revolution was to escape taxation without representation; strong men and women who were willing to trade their lives for self-determined economic benefit guided the westward settlement. China lacks a similar narrative stressing the right of the individual. Neither its people nor its government place the same emphasis on representative government as do Americans. When outsiders write with distrust about China's long-term aspirations for regional hegemony, much of what colors their opinion is a belief that the only good government is a representative one. That the Chinese—both those governing and those governed—do not agree is an always present misunderstanding that Dragon Slayers in particular struggle to internalize.

Like China, America endured a terrible civil war. In America the two issues at the root of the conflict were slavery and the right for a majority of states to mandate laws a minority of states disagreed with. The questions cut to the heart of the American experiment with federalism. The disagreements over states' rights were central to the ideals we claimed to have been founded on, the most general ideals of human liberty, freedom, and equality as well as the balance of powers between the federal and state governments. In contrast to this, China's civil war was the byproduct of a feudal system aging into antiquity, fragmenting, and leaving a leadership vacuum in its wake.

Some 625,000 Americans died during the American Civil War; estimates of Chinese deaths during their civil war range widely, but most agree the number exceeded 1 million.[10] America's civil war ushered in a new era of prosperity commonly referred to as the Gilded Age. Marked by what historians call the Second Industrial Revolution, a newly confident American federation solidified its hold on the American West through an enormous expansion of the nation's railways. No such productive economic and political critical mass awaited China on the other side of its disastrous civil war. In the aftermath of the Chinese Civil War, the country teetered on the edge of political recrimination, famine, and conflict for decades. In the United States, as terrible and destructive as the Civil War was, it resulted in enough clarity that America's economic growth could reignite.

This difference also explains why China is wary of pursuing too much political reform too quickly. It wants the various factions in the country to have a vested interest in stability before it sets additional political reform in motion. As Beijing sees it, too much reform before the country is ready actually increases the likelihood they will get the reform wrong, and set in motion another unnecessary revolution. Because economic growth makes it easier to get buy-in, Beijing believes a good economy is essential to its political stability and development. China's economic growth remains the primary vehicle of its legitimacy. This idea has remained a consistent part of China's philosophy even as it has accelerated investment into the domestic economy, resulting in rates of growth never before seen in human history.

WARP-SPEED MODERNIZATION

Economists have different approaches on how best to compare the economies of the United States and China, but on this point they largely agree: at current projections, no country will come to account for the majority of world trade as fast as China has. As part of an article for *The Economist*, Angus Maddison looked at a history of the world's GDP from 1000 to 2008. He wanted to understand the rise and fall of the world's various great powers over the last thousand years. Maddison found that China and India had accounted for the bulk of the world's GDP from 1 ad to 1700 ad. But he also found that America's GDP, essentially nonexistent in 1700, had by 1870 matched the GDP of the United Kingdom, and by 1900 had overtaken it. It took around two hundred years for the American colonies to outproduce the British Commonwealth.[11]

Another similar measurement was made by Arvind Subramanian at the Peterson Institute for International Economics, who found it took slightly over one hundred years for the United States' economic dominance to rank in the world's top three; in 1870 the largest economy (measured by percentage share of global economic power) was the United Kingdom, followed by Germany and France. In 1973 it was the United States, Japan, and Germany. He forecasts that by 2030 China will have risen to the top, followed by the United States and India.[12] Roughly speaking, China is trying to accomplish in about fifty years what it took the United States almost two hundred to accomplish. As China's polluted rivers and smog-laden cities attest, this is not all good news. But it does support this truth: no country has ever built a comprehensive industrial base as quickly as China. Ever. More than any other difference between the United States and China, it is the speed with which China modernized that distinguishes China's experience from ours. Panda Huggers believe China's modernization program has accomplished at warp speed what America was able to do on cruise control. This means that many of China's problems around environmental pollution should be understood as a byproduct of a country moving at a velocity the modern world has never before seen.

U.S. economic development occurred largely in concert with the Industrial Revolution. As the United States expanded westward, entirely new technologies were developing. These would range from advancements in the field of agriculture to power generation and transportation. In 1794 when Eli Whitney developed the cotton gin, he ushered in a new era of mechanized agriculture. Whitney's machine sparked a wave of similar inventions ranging from Cyrus McCormick's wheat reaper (1834) to John Deere's steel plow (1837). These were massively disruptive advancements: no longer were large farm families necessary for raising crops. Instead, one man could do the work of ten. This freed large segments of the American workforce for other pursuits. Thankfully, America had large swaths of land that needed to be settled, which helped to make absorption of this labor possible. For those less inclined to look westward for their fortunes, other industries were developing in America, many for the first time anywhere.

Agriculture was not the only thing being mechanized; during this period humans were learning to harness the power of steam for transportation. By 1775 James Watt had demonstrated that steam could be used to drive both ships and railcars, powering America's expansion westward into a part of the country that was not only sparsely inhabited but also rich in natural resources. Almost one hundred years after America's Revolutionary War, Andrew Carnegie saw the value of consolidating the American steel industry. He brought an eye for efficiency gains and new technologies that by 1889 made the United States a larger producer of iron than the United Kingdom, where the industry had been started. It was not lost on the steel magnates in the United Kingdom at the time that it had taken the upstart Americans only forty years to go from having no meaningful steel industry to having more capacity and better capabilities than they did. Part of the advantage was American drive and ingenuity, but what likely gave the steel industry in the United States an advantage was that the steel infrastructure in the United States was entirely new. When the United States began to pursue this sector, it built the newest and best-in-class factories, a parallel we are seeing with China today in industries as divergent as clean coal plants, telecommunications, and the electrical grid. If this all sounds similar to the United States' experience with China, it should. This is precisely what Panda Huggers are sensitive to: China is doing to the United States what the United States did to Britain. This process cannot be resisted; it is essential to progress.

But China's modernization is not all a blessing. China's land holdings are nowhere near as generous as the United States. This has translated to basic problems that Panda Huggers believe Dragon Slayers do not fully consider when thinking about China's growth challenges. From 1800 to 1900, America's total land holdings increased roughly 4 times (from 864,746 square miles to 3,547,314). Population increased roughly 13 times (from 5,308,483 to 76,212,168). Simply because of the disproportionate increase in the amount of available land, population density only increased slightly over 3 times, from 6.1 persons per square mile to 21.5. This was America's path of economic development: a thirteenfold increase in population, a fourfold increase in land, and a threefold increase in population density. During this same period America's economic output grew to roughly equal that of the United Kingdom. This sparse population density and rich land resources still characterize the United States in 2017.

Compare this to China, which has grown from a population of 583 million in 1953 to a population of over 1.3 billion (and adding 12–13 million people a year) 58 years later. As a point of comparison, the U.S. Census Bureau estimates that America's population—at current trends—will max out at around 392 million people in 2050. By that time China's population growth will have slowed and maxed out at around 1.5 billion.[13] Keep in mind that, absent an attempt by China to enlarge its territories, in 2050 China will exist within 3,722,029 square miles on which it must support its 1.5 billion people. America will at that same point in time have only 392 million people and hold 3,717,813 square miles. Think of it this way: today, the United States has one-quarter the population of China with more arable land from which to grow its own food.

Even this does not paint the whole picture: America's land holdings constitute some of the world's most arable; 18 percent of America's total land can be farmed. In contrast to this, China's arable land holdings amount to at best 15 percent of its total, with much of this now too contaminated by industrial pollutants to farm. China has 22 percent of the world's population and only 10 percent of the world's arable land. America evolved and grew its population in concert with the industrial age, expanding into largely uninhabited territories at the same time new manufacturing technologies came of age. China has no such luxury. It greets modernity with a profound need to industrialize as quickly as possible and has no comparable undeveloped territories upon which it can direct its millions to settle and farm (and it is this fear that many Dragon Slayers believe will lead China to become a destabilizing expansionary force in search of new farmland to control).

China's economic development is occurring long after the Industrial Revolution and at a time when the countries who mastered the industrial age have largely turned their attention away from heavy industry toward high technology and services. China has been willing to serve as the world's factory precisely when the developed world decided it did not believe manufacturing was the future. As the West doubled down on high technology, health care and financial services, China built its industrial infrastructure as fast as possible. China embraced modern industrialization, developing the sort of manufacturing infrastructure in thirty years it took the United States over one hundred to build. This sort of velocity on China's part was poorly matched to parallel developments in China's environmental and regulatory frameworks. China's economic development has become the ultimate good its leaders can pursue. Finally, they had an answer to the question that had vexed Mao: how could they bring the rural poor into the modern age? The answer was not political ideology; rather, it was pragmatic policy oriented around manufacturing.

SIZE MATTERS

Panda Huggers assert one other important point: China's demographics are so troublesome that it is nearly impossible for the country to become a global power. They are quick to point out that among China's most pressing difficulties as it modernizes are its demographics. Yes, China is getting very rich, very fast, but it is also getting very old just as quickly. China will get older faster than any other rising power in the history of the world. Writing about the challenges China's rapid aging posed, a Center for Strategic and International Studies analysis shows that "in 2005, there were just 16 elderly Chinese for every 100 working-age adults. This aged dependency ratio is due to double to 32 by 2025, then double again to 61 by 2050. By the mid-2020s, China will be adding 10 million elders to its population each year, even as it loses 7 million working-age adults."[14] The government is concerned that, as they have said many times publicly, "China will grow old before it grows rich."[15] This is in marked contrast to Japan and the United States, who both were able to grow rich before they grew old. China faces a serious problem relative to its aging population. Commonly referred to as the 4:2:1 problem, this denotes that each working Chinese adult must care for his or her two parents and their four grandparents.[16] Chinese Confucian culture places high emphasis on familial responsibility with a major expectation that the younger generation will provide a home for its elderly parents and grandparents as they grow old and need care.

Consider the marked difference between China and the United States regarding demographics: during the earliest years of the American republic, families were encouraged to grow larger. Immigration was encouraged. Westward settlements had hundreds of thousands of acres to hunt and farm from, along with natural resources to extract. China's recent growth has none of these luxuries: its territories are limited, and its natural resources—whether oil, water, or arable land—are not enough. These differences drive many of the policies China pursues that Americans find odious. This is why China races to Africa and Venezuela for oil, why until recently it had maintained an onerous one-child policy, and why it pursues economic growth with such single-minded focus. Panda Huggers point out that China's demographics closely parallel those of Asia's 5 billion people spread across India and Indonesia. Other Asian governments are closely watching China's policies because they share many of the same problems.

While China's population is anticipated to peak at around 1.5 billion, India's is expected to peak at 1.7 billion (some birth-rate projections suggest this could reach upwards of 2 billion depending on the policies India's government puts in place). The economic and social challenges of these demographics are unsettling: they will place enormous pressure on still-developing countries and on the infrastructure for health and social care. Several years ago, during an interview for an *Asia Times* column, I asked Chandran Nair, the author of *Consumptionomics*, what the implications for Asia's governments—not limited to China alone—would be if they could not develop policies that would address their demographic challenges. His response is worth quoting at length:

> The consequences will make the Arab Spring look like a walk in the park. I think many—if not most—have misunderstood the source of the Arab revolts. People need access to the basics, and they couldn't get those, which is what precipitated the pushback. They want clean water, and they don't want to have to bring water back in a bucket from a community well; they want reliable electricity and they know their country should be able to provide these basics. And because their governments have sadly been negligent in providing those things, the revolts happened. Of course there are political reasons too. The disenfranchised in Asia have very similar needs: in Asia there are now more people with mobile phones than sanitary toilets. In these cities there are huge amounts of people whose aspirations are not being met. The opportunity and risk for Asian governments is huge. The population in Asia is three billion going on five billion over the next 30 years. There are more poor people in India alone than in all of Africa. Their future is going to depend on whether they can get access to the basics: food, water (for agriculture, subsistence, and sanitation), education, public health and housing. If China and India understand this and adopt policies to provide these to their populations they will be successful.[17]

What those like Nair recognize is that America's development was historically unique. As Nair puts it, "capitalism was borne out of circumstances of abundance and of entitlement. It all looked possible in the West as it had access to vast resources via its colonies and the only challenge was how to export it. Much of our concepts of productivity were built on underpricing resources, simply because there was so much and so few people to use it."[18] Nair's analysis of capitalism draws out one point: the West's development was a historical anomaly China will not enjoy. Given that some 60 percent of all the world's population lives in the Asia-Pacific region, this anomaly improperly understood could precipitate the sort of conflict and famine one shudders to contemplate.

Panda Huggers believe that the challenge for China, and the rest of the world as well, is to recognize that China's economic wealth does not necessarily equate to its readiness to lead the world. The questions it must face are, in many ways, more complex and potentially catastrophic than the questions American leaders in the early to mid-1800s faced. The hard edge of famine, war, and feudalism are in China's recent past. As such, they play a central role in the government's pursuit of economic gain as a means of heading off the most basic of demographic problems.

Like individuals, nations make mistakes. Some of these are minor and easily corrected; others are not. Many times the latter require political brinksmanship or civil war to resolve. The United States has certainly not always been above this, and neither will be China. The much-lauded freedom of the individual to participate in a government of his choosing, this idea which Americans hold so dear and which they believe China should aspire to equally, was not always perfectly executed in the United States. These American freedoms have only existed for several decades if you are an African American, and around one hundred years if you are a woman. This is not to say that given time China will come to similar conclusions and that, as such, the world should be confident in the country's path forward. Rather, it is to suggest that America's criticisms of China must keep in mind America's own struggles to match our ideals with the reality of our culture and the historical context when we came of age. The idea of slavery might have been anathema to many of the Founding Fathers, but it took time and terrible conflict for the ideal of emancipation to become a reality. Similarly, how China suppresses dissent internally may strike many in its ruling party today as a necessity they are eager to be free of.

Just as America's own history illustrates, it takes the combination of new leaders and a crisis to open the door to change; China will be no different.

It is critical to remember that Panda Huggers recognize that many of the questions China must face in its fragile condition are questions America may never have to face at all. China cannot feed itself; America not only can but also has the luxury of using agriculture as a tool of foreign policy and economic gain. China lacks not only arable land but also the water to irrigate what little farmland it does have; America really faces these problems only in such areas as the desert cities across Arizona and Nevada, cities whose existence is made possible because of the abundance and easy transportation of clean water.

China has more than one hundred cities with over 1 million inhabitants, and by 2025, it will have more than two hundred cities with more than 1 million inhabitants. The United States has nine such cities.[19] Population-dense urban areas mean China must design policies and manage its growth to ensure it does not find itself with more than two hundred cities with huge populations, extreme income disparities, and the ensuing violence that characterize cities like Rio de Janeiro or Nairobi. Even in 2017 China has several hundred million people who live in rural agrarian settings with roughly 16 percent of its population under the global poverty line. That its policies sometimes overlook environmental concerns or human rights issues should come as no surprise. Both China's leaders and Panda Huggers believe the country faces a stark choice: grow or die. Yet as China pursues its need for growth with unrelenting focus, it intensifies a key disagreement in the West, an increasingly passionate argument over how China has been brought into the global order, and whether or not the West has been naïve in its treatment of a country with the size, scale, and aspirations of China.

4

Colliding Worldviews

"Could the United States and the People's Republic come to blows again? The possibility cannot be excluded. As Kissinger reminds us, war was the result when Germany rose to challenge Britain economically and geopolitically 100 years ago. Moreover, the key factor that brought America and China together in the 1970s—the common Soviet enemy called 'the polar bear'—has vanished from the scene. Old, intractable differences persist over Taiwan and North Korea. What remains is 'Chimerica,' a less-than-happy marriage of economic convenience in which one partner does all the saving and the other does all the spending."

—Niall Ferguson, "Dr. K's Rx for China," *Newsweek*, May 15, 2011

In 1933 H. G. Wells published one of his less well-known science fiction books, *The Shape of Things to Come*. The story is set in a world nearly one hundred years in the future as described by a textbook published, ironically enough, in 2016. The story's protagonist is a well-known diplomat who recalls the textbook through a series of dream-like sequences. In *The Shape of Things to Come*, Wells's projects his aspiration for mankind with wild-eyed enthusiasm: he envisions a world without war, with peace and economic prosperity for all, and with an enlightened citizenry of such nobility and intelligence that the need for government has disappeared. That this is all done through the establishment of a global government, the eradication of religion, and making English the global lingua franca betrays Wells's own biases. But this utopia does not unfold in a linear fashion; no, this world's possibility exists only on the other side of colliding worldviews where mankind's destructive follies are released, on the other side of economic malaise, pestilence, and the resulting chaos.

Wells's book deserves to be read in concert with other writers of his day, people such as Norman Angell and Karel Čapek who were wrestling with how technology and in particular the nature of war and the modern nation-state were going to interact with and inform one another. Angell developed a theory of political science that proved to disastrously underestimate man's shortsightedness, while Čapek explored similar topics through plays and works of fiction that orchestrated a delicate balance between hope and fear. Many of the writers and thinkers from this era sensed that their generation stood at the cusp of a major transition in how governments interacted with their citizens, how technology shaped economies, and how mankind understood itself. They knew a change was coming, and more than a few had an ominous foreboding as to how the established and new worldviews might collide.

Dragon Slayers' and Panda Huggers' only disagreement is not about China. Their opposition to one another goes much deeper and reflects a deep divide in how conservative and progressive political theory is understood and implemented as public policy. Both camps disagree on the role of politics, with Dragon Slayers tending to believe that the state should always be minimized, and Panda Huggers tending to think the state has a role to play. These positions give either camp the upper hand at particular moments of history. Dragon Slayers have something important to say around not looking past the ugly side of China's rise; their view on the dark side of human nature, in particular as it is commonly expressed in politics, has relevance in how the West should view China. But the view of Panda Huggers has its own merits; Panda Huggers choose to believe a better future is possible, provided China progresses with additional liberalization of its political and economic systems (neither of which can be taken for granted). Panda Huggers also recognize that a worldview that requires the other side to break is dangerous in its own way, as political revolutions from the French to the Bolsheviks suggest. There are obvious tensions between these two camps and the interpretations offered here. The point is not to make a pure reductionist argument or argue for the absolute truth of either worldview; rather, it is to encourage reflection on how attitudes toward China can be used and abused by both camps.

The great danger is that China becomes a proxy for deeper disconnects between these two worldviews. Dragon Slayers and Panda Huggers have always been part of the conversation as China has gradually opened and worked to enter the global stage. Nixon was met with cries of derision and suspicion from many within his own party when he first announced America's new policy toward China. As Nixon's presidential library likes to point out, "it was conservatives within the Republican Party who were vexed about his future meeting with communist leaders, and saw it as a betrayal to the U.S.'s long standing ethnic Chinese and democratic ally, Taiwan."[1] One of Nixon's conservative nemeses, Barry Goldwater, infamously said of Nixon's trip to China, "As far as I'm concerned, Nixon can go to China and stay there."[2] During Nixon's presidency, pictures of him morphing into a Chinese man were displayed with the caption "Tricky Dicky." George H. W. Bush's efforts to grant China permanent trade status resulted in angry responses from organized labor and committed human rights advocates who saw China as an untrustworthy authoritarian regime. Clinton's advocacy for China to receive the Most Favored National (MNF) status brought old disagreements between the two camps forward once again. At that time, Republican congressman Christopher Cox channeled bipartisan discomfort with President Clinton's approach to Beijing when he noted, "we will reach the nadir of our abandonment of human rights if Clinton appears at Tiananmen Square."[3]

Beneath the surface of a conversation the United States had about China were four deeper disagreements, ones that continue to play out today in our policies toward countries like Cuba, Iran, and North Korea. First is the disagreement over whether a values-based or realpolitik approach to countries outside of the West's sphere of influence is more likely to bring stability and further advance America's interests. Second is the belief that a policy of inclusion to "outsider" countries, rather than isolation and exclusion, goes further to foster openness and peace. Third is the notion that the United States is in a privileged position and can afford to be generous to the point of trading away some short-term economic security in the interests of bringing a poor, politically backward, and isolated country into the global order. Fourth, and perhaps most significantly, is the disagreement over what creates meaningful change: crisis or conciliation.

VALUES-BASED VERSUS REALPOLITIK

It is important to frame why Nixon was really in China in the first place because it sets the stage for how these contrasting worldviews have been projected into today. Nixon's opening China is largely seen as one of history's best example of realpolitik, the pragmatic execution of foreign policy to further one country's strategic interests over another. The realpolitik approach intentionally looks past value-based disconnects because it believes, among other things, that pursuit of strategic interests rank as a higher priority than pure ideology. Expressed toward China, this has meant that the United States chose to aggressively normalize and economically interact with China even though China remained a Communist country with all manner of human rights abuses, suppression of political dissent, and questionable intentions about the role of government in people's lives.

While the China of 1976 was in deep pain and near-paralysis, the United States had seen better days, though it was definitely not suffering on the scale China was. In America the Nixon administration had emphasized price controls and severed the country from the gold standard, all in a desperate attempt to fight runaway inflation. Oil prices had skyrocketed, which had sent a powerful tremor through the American psyche as the country began to wonder if a future of endless cheap energy could no longer be taken for granted. The stock market had cratered, and with interest rates at what many thought might be permanently high levels, the American Dream of homeownership was quickly falling out of grasp. The war in Vietnam was dragging on, fed by an administration unwilling to be honest with the American people as to where the war was going.

Before Nixon resigned in August of 1974, he set in motion a series of events that would bring China and the United States together. Americans forget why Nixon and his secretary of state Henry Kissinger reached out to

China in the seventies. Anyone surprised to see Nixon's openness toward China could not see past his prior red-baiting for an always pragmatic and strategic politician. Those taken unawares by Nixon's realism had overlooked the 1967 essay in *Foreign Affairs* in which he wrote, "we simply cannot afford to leave China forever outside the family of nations, there to nurture its fantasies, cherish its hates and threaten its neighbors. There is no place on this small planet for a billion of its potentially most able people to live in angry isolation."[4]

Both Nixon and Kissinger spoke publicly about the geopolitical concerns that motivated their efforts to draw China into America's sphere of influence. Nixon's motives were a mix of practical politics and international great-power strategy, what many have called realpolitik. Nixon and Kissinger were also motivated in large part by a desire to see China align itself with the United States against the Soviet Union. Nixon's questionable humanitarian impulses aside, he believed that after China opened to the United States, we would have a regional counterweight to Soviet power in Asia. In addition, Nixon believed if he could get China on friendly terms with the United States, the Soviet Union would be encircled by enemies and at the same time China would stop engaging in the skirmishes with the United States through Chinese-supported Communist insurgencies in the Pacific and Third World countries. Nixon, to his great credit, was proven correct on each of these points.

What would a values-based approach to China in 1972 have looked like? We can assume that much of what constituted our relationship with China and the Soviet Union would have more or less overlapped. To say that differently, we would have treated the two countries in the same way: both as enemies. But would a purely values-based foreign policy toward China have forever kept that country at arm's length, allowing it to struggle forward in the period after Mao's death with only the Soviet Union to turn to? A values-based worldview is not as naïve as some make it out to be. Many who hold to this belief system are concerned that normalized relations with a country whose values are fundamentally at odds with our own runs two risks. First, they fear that such normalized relations will dilute our own appreciation of what makes Western, post-Enlightenment political and moral systems superior. Second, they are concerned that in the act of normalizing relations with a country that does not share our values, we risk empowering the incumbent, status quo powerbrokers in a country like China. If normalization does, as it has in China, enrich and empower totalitarians, we may have done nothing but legitimize them and make it harder for lasting reform to take place.

Values-driven foreign policy can be tricky. At one extreme you end up with the worldview of someone like Noam Chomsky, who in every expression of American realpolitik sees hypocrisy and self-interest above dedication to what he would describe as "supposed" American values of freedom and liberal democracy. At the other extreme you end up with Senator Tom Cotton, who seems willing to go to war with any and every country from the Middle East to the South China Sea who dares to assert a different point of view than what happens to comport to American foreign policy. Both have a certain self-righteous and nearly puritanical streak that understandably makes most people in the moderate middle of American political life uncomfortable.

Since the late seventies, American presidential elections have reflected a value-based approach to U.S.-China relations, while actual governing once the elections are over reflects realpolitik. Nixon was the first presidential candidate to try this tactic: the most prolific red-baiter in American politics since Joseph McCarthy, Nixon suggested in the heat of the 1960 presidential campaign that John F. Kennedy did not possess the values to stand up to Communist China. Then, Nixon's value-based approach backfired on him badly when measured against Kennedy's cool headed realpolitik thinking. As Robert Norris, a writer at *American Diplomacy*, pointed out, "throughout the debates Kennedy reminded the American people that Nixon might actually risk military action to defend Quemoy and Matsu even in the absence of an all-out attack on Taiwan."[5] Since then, American politicians have learned when and where to emphasize values over real-world concerns when talking about U.S.-China relations. Nixon would not be the only Republican or Democratic Presidential candidate to run on the basis of a values-based approach to China, only to turn toward realpolitik when actually governing. Reagan attacked Carter as naïve about China's Communist intentions. George H. W. Bush proved vulnerable to Bill Clinton's attacks on the Bush administration's approach to China after the massacre in Tiananmen, when Clinton said that Bush was "coddling aging rulers with undisguised contempt for democracy, [and] for human rights."[6] Barack Obama dismissed George Bush's policy approach toward China, calling him "a patsy."[7] And, of course, the 2016 presidential election was all sorts of fun in this regard, with then-candidate Donald Trump accusing China of "raping" America.[8]

For several decades American politics has accommodated the disconnect between how presidential candidates talk about China in the middle of an election and how they actually govern. Yet this is the very sort of hypocrisy that Americans now appear ready to ask their politicians to remedy. The track of what American presidential candidates say during an election and the track of how they actually govern have been kept separate—so far, that is. The primal rage that expressed itself in the 2016 presidential election was about many things, but at its roots it was a desire to see the end of politicians' saying one thing in a campaign only to do the opposite in office. The idea that U.S.-China relations as described in campaigns will be forever distinct from what government actually does may no longer be accurate.

A values-based foreign policy is nothing to ridicule. It pays particular attention to times when countries look past human rights abuses or autocratic rulers. Values-driven foreign policy has an important place at the table. At its best, it keeps a democracy honest about the choices it is making. But values-driven foreign policy can also be a convenient way to avoid making hard choices. In a world of gray, which is where politics and foreign policy nearly always live, pure values-driven decisions would have prevented FDR from working with Stalin in World War II, as just one example. This type of moral calculus is very much needed in the age of Trump, when too many Americans have forgotten about the thorny need for discernment. Realpolitik in contrast requires a certain degree of confidence in your situation; American foreign policy after World War II could afford to use triangulation and, in the case of Nixon's realpolitik approach to China, could choose to embrace a former adversary, in large part because the United States was confident in its ability to ultimately beat the Soviet Union. Similarly, realpolitik foreign policy could guide America's approach to China because it had absolute clarity over what could happen if the United States did not figure out a way to contain Soviet influence. Realpolitik's underlying confidence in the superiority of the American way allowed it to take risks and argue for a policy of inclusion instead of exclusion, an approach that seems obvious today but was anything but in the 1970s.

INCLUSION VERSUS EXCLUSION

Not too long ago, America faced this question with China: how do we turn an enemy into a friend? Historically, the answer has many times been found only on the other side of conflict. Why do we need to avoid blaming China for the situation the United States finds itself in? Because what the United States and China have proven is that by turning away from hostility toward peaceful engagement, two countries that once were at violent odds with one another can in fact find common ground. Is the model inadequate? Yes. Did we overlook domestic problems while we engaged China? Yes. Have we been too generous in our evaluations of China's political process? Yes. But we should not lose sight of the fact that whatever grievances we may have with China's current economic policies and political shortcomings, our policy of engagement has turned a country that could well have become another enemy into a friend. In his 2009 Nobel Peace Prize acceptance speech, former president Barack Obama made this point very clearly: "In light of the Cultural Revolution's horrors, Nixon's meeting with Mao appeared inexcusable—and yet it surely helped set China on a path where millions of its citizens have been lifted from poverty and connected to open societies. . . . No repressive regime can move down a new path unless it has the choice of an open door."[9]

How America and China have managed to navigate away from suspicion and animosity toward trust and friendship is one of the great historical achievements of the last seventy years. We easily forget our two countries fought two proxy wars, one in Korea and one in Vietnam. As each ended, the idea of a peaceful and constructive relationship with China seemed impossible and, to many, undesirable. The larger point of how the United States generally engaged China should serve as a lesson for developed nations in how to most peacefully achieve orderly transitions from closed to open societies. Today, the developed world can see in countries like Iran and North Korea a similar problem: how do we turn isolated and hostile powers away from destructive behavior toward a productive engagement with the rest of the world?

Whatever we might think about the leaders of these countries, it is not in our interests to shed blood or to see their countries collapse. The leaders of both Iran and North Korea are evil individuals, capable of wanton acts of cruelty and terrorism to protect their tenuous grasp on power. Yet what would happen in the Middle East if the Iranian government collapsed? What might occur in the countries surrounding North Korea, like China, South Korea ,and Japan, if Pyongyang implodes? As President Trump has learned, there are no good choices when it comes to North Korea. The human costs would be enormous, especially in the latter case of an implosion of Pyongyang. The question must be asked: how confident are we that the ultimate outcome of either scenario would be a more stable world?

A policy of inclusion proposes that the United States is most likely to achieve our desired ends if we set aside differences and seek dialogue with our enemies. This school of thought put forward the policy of engagement that has knit the United States and China together since Kissinger. Engagement is still the framework within which we work together today. It served to inform President Obama, who during his first Democratic presidential primary was asked whether he would sit down and meet with leaders of countries long hostile to America. His answer was classic realism-engagement: he would be willing to do so "without preconditions."[10] While conservatives (and his Democratic opponent Hillary Clinton) lashed out at this as naïve, Obama had simply echoed the policy framework that has served as the foundation during U.S.-China relations for the last four decades.

Inclusion is under attack today precisely because the policy does not appear to be working as quickly as some pundits would like, in particular with North Korea and Iran. Writing in a February 2010 edition of *Foreign*

Policy, James Traub noted with respect to the Obama administration's emphasis on engagement with Iran that while it might be the most viable option, it was also a deeply unsatisfying one: "Simple policies, like Bush's Freedom Agenda, afford immediate gratification—and then deep disappointment down the road. Nuanced, many-things-at-once policies require patience and a tolerance for ambiguous victories. We now have abundant evidence that this is not a patient or tolerant moment. You have to wonder how long complicated can survive in the absence of big wins."[11] While the validity of engagement as a central part of America's foreign policy can be most easily questioned relative to our relationship with Iran and North Korea, the same misgivings are beginning to color our relationship with China.

In his *Foreign Policy* essay, Traub touches on the much deeper question of whether inclusion is under attack because of domestic political pressures. Even though our relationship with China is more mature and stable and less contentious than our relationship with either Iran or North Korea, many remain unsure whether engagement with any of these countries is right. Politicians who, as one pundit once remarked, have "a Parkinsonian grasp on history" are forever afraid that they will extend an olive branch to an enemy, only to find they have badly misjudged their opponent, ensuring they become the Neville Chamberlain of their day. Chamberlain, the British prime minister in the run-up to World War II, infamously met with Hitler and secured what he believed to be the German fuhrer's word that there would never be war between the two countries, what Chamberlain called "peace for our time." The ensuing war Hitler set in motion violated the agreement Chamberlain brought home from Munich and utterly emasculated his political credibility back in the UK. Even today politicians have taken note not to make the same mistake, which is always one of the concerns they bring to the table when the policy of engagement with an adversary is discussed.

In 2017 the American policy of inclusion with China has critics who take this lesson to heart. Largely populated by Dragon Slayers, this group of critics believes the "real" China is best seen in Tiananmen and the continuing repression of individual freedoms. Incidents like those recently surrounding the blind dissident Chen Guangcheng or the artist Ai Wei-wei reinforce the bad impression Dragon Slayers have about China. For Dragon Slayers what we are doing with China through our policy of engagement accommodates and enriches authoritarians. Long-standing misgivings from this group have been amplified in recent years, as the American economy has struggled and it has become easier—and even more politically valuable—to draw into question whether engaging China is any longer a wise strategy.

China faced two critical moments during the last fifty years: immediately after the reforms of the late seventies and in the aftermath of Tiananmen. Had the United States been less willing to include China into the global order, it is likely the country would have fallen into chaos. We may take China's openness to the West for granted now, but in the late seventies China could have slipped, turning inwards and folding in on itself. Things in China could have gone very differently, and they almost did. In the period after Mao died, the so-called Gang of Four, whose ideas were aligned with those of the most disastrous elements of the Cultural Revolution, vied to fill the power vacuum left in Mao's wake. Even after having defeated the Gang of Four, a bloodless coup was necessary to once and for all break from the Maoist model and embrace the market reforms Deng Xiaoping advocated. The China seen today is the result of this fight for control having been won by advocates of the American economic model. As China's post-Mao leaders proceeded to open their economy to foreign investment and to encourage entrepreneurship within their own people, they were timidly walking down the path of reform that America had long advocated.

Beyond whether they should continue with Mao's failed policies or pursue America's free market model, China's leadership could have embraced reforms designed to emulate the economy of the Soviet Union. Given what we know now about the decay of the Soviet Union's economic system, that may seem unlikely; however, in the late seventies and early eighties, the Soviet model was still widely perceived to be a viable alternative to the American model. *Glasnost* was years away. The Soviet Union of the late seventies and early eighties was a muscular bear, making its regional aspirations felt in Afghanistan and enabling conflicts with the United

States through various proxies around the world. To many outside the Soviet Union, the Warsaw Pact was widely understood to be a feared and effective fighting force, capable of acting with real offensive power in ways that could cripple western Europe.

Why did China not find the model of the Soviet Union more attractive than that of the United States? Surely following the Soviet way would have been more consistent with China's recent past. Chinese chairman Hua Guofeng, one of Deng Xiaoping's rivals for power after Mao's death, believed China should pursue a more Soviet model versus the more Western model Deng advocated for. China was one of the rare countries in the world with good access to both the Soviet Union and the United States. Because of this, China was able to look at both countries through many lenses: economic, cultural, military and political. China made the choice to approximate the American economic model.

A similar choice awaited China in the weeks after Tiananmen Square. China's leadership chose to enact martial law and clamp down on the protesters in and around Tiananmen. The long-standing priority the party has given to social order made the decision all but inevitable, a reality the more than one thousand people who died must have understood. In this same way, the easy choice in the weeks following Tiananmen would have been to wall the country off from outsiders, retrench from the tentative economic reforms it had begun, and settle into an uneasy and uncertain path from which additional changes would not be possible. But China's leadership did not take this path. Instead, China's leadership offered an exchange with the Chinese people: you will get access to a new world of economic opportunities, but only if you agree to live and work within the confines established by the party.

Today we may find the status of China's reforms process inadequate and incomplete. We have to remember not only where China is coming from but more importantly the choices it has made between a path it knew well (Communism) and a path no one knows well (the blended socialist-capitalist model they now find themselves with). In both of these pivotal moments—Deng's reforms and the period immediately after Tiananmen—China's leadership chose to step away from a model that was most comfortable toward a model that was aligned with America's values and policies. We may take these decisions for granted today, but in the moments when they occurred, the world had no such certainty. China could have just as easily pivoted inwards, choosing to further isolate themselves as North Korea has continued to do and as Iran did after its shah was deposed.

AMERICA CAN AFFORD TO BE GENEROUS

Donald Trump is not the first American president to lay waste to the previous White House staff and diplomatic core. In the aftermath of Andrew Jackson's hotly contested 1829 presidential election, the new American president replaced an unprecedented number of appointed government officials from the previous administration with those loyal to him. The incoming administration turned over nearly 10 percent of all appointed offices with those swearing allegiance to Jackson's Democrats. Responding to public outcry over such blatant patronage, New York Senator William Marcy casually responded, "to the victor goes the spoils." The message was simple: we won, and we get to make the rules. In a similar sense, America won its two major conflicts of the last hundred years: World War II and the Cold War. As victor the United States was entitled to the spoils. As part of those spoils, the United States could drive the rules that knit the world together in the aftermath of both World War II and the Cold War. Rulemaking bodies like the IMF and WTO are largely constructs of American power, and their initial legitimacy owes a real debt to American power and policy.

Economically, victory after World War II left the United States the unassailable strongman. Our manufacturing output amounted to over 50 percent of the world's total, which enriched our coffers and laid the groundwork for many American multinational companies who dominate the world's economy today. Beyond the economic gains, the American culture, way of life, and political ideas were elevated to ideals—standards they richly deserved. American movies exported a vision of what it was like to live in America, admittedly with Hollywood's own spin. American products were the best a middle-class American would ever aspire to own and enjoy. American politics put forward a vision that government was empowered by the consent of its citizens, that personal freedom was an absolute necessity, and that such freedom was integral to economic growth. All of this resulted in an attitude, which culminated in the nineties, that America could afford to be generous toward countries like China, that we could accommodate their ideological differences as eccentricities and choose to do business with them.

In the midst of the United States' current economic anxieties, it is easy to lose sight of the fact that the world we live in is a world we created. Relative to China, this is especially important to understand: China's path forward was heavily influenced by America's efforts to engage the country, using a combination of threats, coercion, and incentives to encourage China to leave Mao's perverted form of government behind and embrace the free market. We may feel today they have come up short of the ideal, but our criticism of their shortcomings needs to reflect both what China and the West more broadly should have done differently. We now feel China has been the main beneficiary of our policies since the peace dividend; however, it is worth considering that our overall strategy was too heavily weighted toward policies that would help China and too lightly weighted toward those matters within our own country that would be shaped by China's presence in the globalized economy.

This period also marks a moment when America's political class demonstrated a spectacular lack of imagination and vision over how China's entry to the world's system of trade would impact American workers and the domestic economy. In hindsight, our policies were almost Pollyannaish, with too much focus on the upside potential and too little time, energy, or focus spent on downside risks or envisioning ways to mitigate these effects on American workers and industry. Regardless, the simple reality is that China is where it is today in no small part because it so closely followed the policies we asked it to.

CRISIS OR CONCILIATION

The final colliding worldview is between those who believe change is only possible in the aftermath of a crisis and those who believe that history suggests crises many times spiral out of control unnecessarily and as such prefer policies that pursue conciliation. To the credit of those who hold to the belief in crisis-driven change, much of what we know about human nature supports this. Having watched the world he knew tear itself apart during the First World War, the Austrian economist Joseph Schumpeter developed the idea of "creative destruction." He believed that complex political economies of a certain size were only able to deal with long-standing structural problems once they had collapsed in on themselves, a process that destroyed the status quo and allowed new ideas to emerge that could obtain enough political support to be seen through into actual policy. Schumpeter's view of what is required for change is painful, but it does reflect something essential about human nature. It also informs those who believe a country's enemies should be allowed to collapse before negotiating with them (the conservative view of Cuba, Iran, and North Korea), or that businesses should have been allowed to fail in the middle of the 2008 financial crisis. Within certain parts of the American foreign policy community, for their suspicions about China to proven right would require the country to collapse.

Those who would believe that countries like China should be forced to live separate from the world and allowed to collapse due to their political ideologies are willing to believe two things that China's leadership does not. First, they can believe that such a collapse would end well for the Chinese people, and second, that a collapse in China would not also destabilize the country's neighbors. The misgivings of China's Communist Party have to do with its ability to transition from a poor, underdeveloped and uneducated country to a modern economy with a viable middle class. In many ways the conflict between America and China over the question of how China should liberalize boils down to a disagreement over the speed and form by which China should adjust its authoritarian policies. China's unwillingness to move faster in the areas of human rights and accommodating dissent is more a function of insecurity over its ability to make the jump from agrarian to modern economy than it is a fundamental predisposition to excluding the average Chinese citizen from the political process.

Yes, there are hard-liners in Chinese politics who harbor desires to remake the world in Mao's image and who want to rule over the country in much the same way he did, but these are a distinct minority. The monolithic nature of the party's face to the world many times obscures the diversity of opinions within, a diversity that in many cases could shed light on the question of how quickly and in what ways China's political institutions might change. Many in China's political class believe the country is predisposed to instability and that China's history suggests it can easily break into warring factions. Because they believe this instability is enabled by lack of education and access to economic opportunity and by social injustices, Beijing asserts that its strong hand is necessary to help the Chinese. Many of the best China hands have begun to use harsher words about China's political reforms. The unfortunate reality is that China is not liberalizing as we thought they would. Some of this is a reflection on our frustrations over not seeing China as far along as we thought they should be. Some of the reasons why China is slowing the process of reform are that within the party there is a fear they are close to losing control. China's leaders know how far they have come and how fast, and they are more aware than we are of the problems this creates.

China's hard-liners fear losing control over the country because it would break their hope for a Chinese "Communist" century; moderates fear losing control over the country because it could set the country back to its feudal past; both camps fear losing control in general. On this point it is essential to hold two ideas in equal tension: China's authoritarian rulers want the status quo maintained so they can hold onto power for their own profit, but equally China's authoritarian rulers want the status quo maintained so they can prevent the country from sliding into chaos and anarchy, potentially setting the country back to where it was in the thirties. These are both prevalent ideas within Chinese politics, and determining which is more dominant in the moment is incredibly difficult.

In December 2011 an estimated twenty thousand villagers in Wukan took to the streets to protest the death of a political activist at the hands of local police.[12] Their anger was not only at his unlawful imprisonment and subsequent beating but at the ongoing practice of local Chinese municipalities' appropriating land from villagers. Local leaders were able to tamp down the protests and made promises to better compensate villagers for land taken through eminent domain claims; however, the protests exposed the tension between the heavy-handed actions by the authoritarian Chinese government and the benefits derived from these steps for the average Chinese. These frustrations are not going away and are likely to grow over the coming years. It remains one of the many ways China's political system could topple.

If Americans and Europeans have a role to play in this back-and-forth between China's two political camps, it is preventing anarchy. Revolutions are messy things, and China's history of revolutions should present a specific lesson on how badly things could go for the Chinese if the country were to collapse. The China of today in few ways parallels the America of Revolutionary War days. Americans who want to see China adopt increasingly democratic forms of government must swallow the bitter pill that China's path forward will not look like ours; in fact, it will diverge in ways we are going to find uncomfortable and disconcerting. The cycle of Beijing tightening up controls, then relaxing them only to tighten them up again is going to be a long-standing frustration for those who want to see China give itself over to democratic governance. The larger question for Americans is how we engage China during these periods of tightening. Ideally, we should be able to point the Chinese toward the positive results of our particular form of governance. This is obviously a point few Americans would be comfortable making today, given the haphazard state of American politics and the disappointing outcomes for average people it has created.

China does have many problems that could lead to collapse. For critics like many Dragon Slayers, if the country's growth were to slow, or if their property markets were to crater, or if a bad debt problem were to create a structural financial crisis, that would validate that the Chinese model is not better than the Western economic and political systems. But the idea that China needs to collapse in order for America's political economy to be validated is dangerous. China is not entirely alone in dealing with questions of how to modernize its economy, compete globally, and deal with the need to make massive investments in social services and health care. During our lifetimes, the world will encounter one of our greatest tests yet: we must find a way for two countries, each with over a billion people to take care of, to modernize their economies and evolve their political systems without upending the established order. These two countries are India and China. In neither should we assume their ability to meet these challenges is certain. History warns us that we can, and often do, underestimate our need to proactively think through the downside risks that the world faces. This is particularly the case in the midst of moments of historical hubris (at the end of the Cold War) and technical utopian thinking (right now, when technology is clearly going to be equally freeing and damaging to many). If China and India in particular cannot rise to meet these challenges and deliver meaningful improvements in quality of life for their people, the negative effects will not be limited to their countries; they will be felt all the way to the American heartland.

What happens to China in the midst of an economic and political crisis? Three scenarios are possible. First, China's crisis coincides with a political revolution that brings the Western ideas of dissent and representative government into vogue. In the second scenario, China's implosion drives the country inwards, walling itself off from the rest of the world but leaving the party in power. It sounds improbable until we remember that China has done precisely this on numerous occasions throughout its history. The country's size makes the argument that it can "go it alone" an easy one for people to latch onto in the midst of a crisis, in particular one precipitated by ominous language from its trading partners. Third, a crisis in China could trigger anarchy. The scope of this anarchy could go well beyond anything Americans can ponder. China's past of breaking into fragmented pieces ruled by warlords is not so long ago. In this environment, the country could go to war with itself, setting in motion another round of recriminations, famine, and civil war the likes it has not seen since the thirties.

Those who advocate for a crisis that would lead to collapse also tend to be those who took a hard line in Iraq and who still struggle to admit that the collapse of an already dysfunctional nation-state such as Iraq can destabilize the region in ways that make the resulting world even more dangerous. Just as in Saddam Hussein's Iraq, Mao's China was a country with a governance system built around cronies and sycophants. Whatever competent system of government once existed within either of these countries had long been robbed of its legitimacy. Both countries had evolved political cultures that reflected praise and adulation back to their supreme leader rather than emphasizing policies that would benefit their countries. While China may not have had a recent history of sectarian violence like Iraq, it does have a recent history of violent civil war. Both countries have predispositions to violence, admittedly for different reasons. The world can now see with terrible clarity how badly things went as Iraq crumbled. For all the hand-wringing over how Iraq's collapse has destabilized the region, it is worth considering what the Asia-Pacific region would look like if China had collapsed in the nineties, or if it were to do so today. China's leadership understands this much better than anyone else, and it is the defining central truth that animates their policies. Understanding China's choices is essential if we are to place particular emphasis on either the Dragon Slayer's or the Panda Hugger's proposed approach to China.

THREE CHOICES

The worldviews of both Panda Huggers and Dragon Slayers recognize that the China of the late seventies and the China of today share three choices. They could undergo a political revolution. Here the two camps differ on what would have happened, with the Panda Huggers believing such an event would have driven the country into chaos, and the Dragon Slayers believing revolution—while messy—would have given rise to a more democratic China. Or the country could have collapsed in a sort of anarchy analogous to the civil war of the thirties. China could have ceased to exist as we know it. While this may seem outlandish today, it is a possibility that has historic parallels in the country over the last several hundred years. Or China could gradually reform. At various times both camps have been willing to give this theory credibility; however, Panda Huggers still view it as the most likely path forward while Dragon Slayers are no longer comfortable thinking the gradual path is going to do anything but enrich the Chinese Communist Party.

There are a couple of different ways to look at these three choices. One views these three choices as both historical and contemporary problems: everything old is new again. This view says that this particular set of challenges has always been and will always be unique to China. In particular on the question of how China would react to political revolution, the two camps agree that China's ability to withstand another political revolution and come out the other side with a stable and prodemocracy government was unlikely through the late seventies and late eighties; however, where the two camps differ is on whether this problem still exists. Panda Huggers tend to view China's many problems—their income inequality, history of collapse and political turmoil, famine, and economic misery—and believe the world cannot overlook the fragility of Chinese society, even today. While Panda Huggers may blanch at Beijing's most recent reversal on its practices of political dissent, they choose to believe that on the whole China's policy makers recognize their need to reform and will do so gradually.

In contrast to this are Dragon Slayers, who believe China's civil society, while having its share of unique problems and blind spots, is capable of much more aggressive political reform than Panda Huggers acknowledge. Dragon Slayers have a heightened notion of what democracy brings to society and are rightfully suspicious of leaders or governments who put forward the idea that those in power have the right—or perhaps as Beijing would say, the responsibility—to abrogate individual rights in the public's interest. For Dragon Slayers Beijing's efforts in these areas show an underlying distrust of human nature. Dragon Slayers place more trust in a current-day political revolution in China that would break Beijing's grip on power because they believe the Chinese can be trusted with their own freedom and because they view crises as a necessary cleansing act every country must go through. If echoes of this argument seem familiar, they should: it was a similar argument made about Iraq specifically and the Middle East in general. As these situations have continued to make plain to the world, there are other factors within a society that determine its ability to be ready for democracy. While we may applaud the Dragon Slayers' elevated notion of the human ideal, Panda Huggers want to ground these aspirations in the reality of China's anarchic past. The two sides fundamentally differ on the question of how China would react to a political revolution.

Regardless of whether Panda Huggers or Dragon Slayers are ultimately proven right about China, the reality of U.S.-China relations over the last thirty years has been a powerful statement on the possibility that two countries once hostile toward one another can find a way to open and engage. America not only won the Cold War but it peacefully provoked a hostile world power to make substantial changes to its economy, internal political systems, and orientation to the world's rule sets in a way that avoided bloodshed. This is an accomplishment of historic proportions, yet Americans have lost sight of just what our leadership and the twin foreign policies of realism and engagement have proved. China owes much of its success to policies America embodied and advocated. That we now feel threatened and insecure by China's rise is a terrible misreading of the enormous success tying our two countries together.

CAN WE TRUST CHINA?

Much of the disagreement over which worldview more accurately applies to China—whether Panda Huggers or Dragon Slayers are more right about the direction of China's reform process—is at its root a question of trust. Said most simply, can we trust China? Trust is not an absolute. We should feel comfortable answering this question conditionally. Can we trust the China of 2017 more than we could trust China's leadership in the years immediately following Mao's death? Yes, we can trust today's leadership more. They have honored many of the obligations they encountered as part of joining the international order. The economic reforms they have made—while still coming up short of all those we might have liked to see—are nonetheless impressive. These changes point in the overall direction of liberalization rather than collectivization. While problems with corruption and income inequality are pervasive in the country, few countries in modern history have done as much to lift the average citizen from poverty as has the leadership of the Chinese Communist Party.

Trust and loyalty are dangerous concepts to confuse with one another. Our trust of China is not the same thing as being loyal to China. Some Panda Huggers who have historically been loyal to the country and who want to believe the best about its leadership are now becoming more critical over recent tightening on political dissent by China's Communist

Party. For many in this camp, Beijing's reaction to Liu Xiaobo's winning the 2010 Nobel Peace Prize for "his long and non-violent struggle for human rights in China," the jailing of Chinese artist Ai Weiwei, and the abuse of Chen Guangcheng signal a country whose political reforms may have either stalled out temporarily or are under more fundamental assault from hard-liners within the party. These situations, coupled with the government's gross overreaction to the threat of what critics of the Chinese government hoped would be a "Jasmine Revolution" in the months immediately following the 2011 Arab Spring, have led some Panda Huggers to realize they may need to back away from past loyalties with China's leadership and begin putting additional qualifications on the relationship between the two countries.

President Ronald Reagan made famous the maxim "trust, but verify" in his discussions with Mikhail Gorbachev. Interestingly enough, it took an American president to make this Russian proverb originally coined by Vladimir Lenin famous ("doveryai, no proveryai")! The sentiment captured the tenuous balancing act between the United States and the Soviet Union in those uncertain days when it was unclear whether the two would find common ground. Similarly, the maxim has value today as the United States casts an increasingly suspicious eye toward China. Can we trust the country to ultimately reform its political system and further open its economy? The answer cannot be a simple "yes" or "no"; rather, as Reagan suggested, it must be conditional on how China responds to the changing landscape domestically and internationally. The challenge here for U.S. policy is to avoid blaming China for problems in America and by doing so harm China's ability to further reform.

This sort of rebalancing act will be a delicate process that is sure to anger stakeholders in China and the United States. For the United States, Panda Huggers and Dragon Slayers are going to come away disappointed with the ultimate shape of China's reforms. China will not be democratic enough for Panda Huggers to feel that their past loyalty has been rewarded, and the country will be too socialistic for Dragon Slayers to trust the country's leadership. For China a rebalancing would require it to acknowledge internally that the globalization that benefited China for much of the last several decades has also dislocated many jobs in the West. These jobs were held by a once-vibrant middle class in the United States and Europe, and as such, their loss is being severely felt today by their respective domestic political systems. As a consequence of this, China's future economic growth is going to have to develop a domestic consumption-based economy. Beijing will also have to make sure it remains open to foreign multinationals who need access to China's growing market to sustain the revenue losses they face as their domestic markets continue to struggle.

As outsiders, understanding China's path forward likely relies heavily on what its economic reforms signal to the world about the country's long-term political reforms. Both worldviews agree political reform becomes more likely, though not inevitable, as countries around the world become reliant on the free market. Regardless of what Beijing's intentions are, the longer it signals a willingness to subject its own economy to international rule sets like those embodied by the WTO, the more these adjustments suggest to outsiders that China's reform process will jump from being a purely economic affair to one with political implications as well. In this limited sense, China has the hope of again earning the trust of disaffected Panda Huggers by showing that the country's current backslide in the area of human rights was a temporary adjustment.

The virtuous cycle that knit the United States and China together—where China's economy took jobs Americans did not want and made products less expensively—now threatens to become a death spiral. The idea that two disparate worldviews, one encouraging conciliation and the other competition, could coexist in a way that ultimately drove sound policy forward has all but disappeared. As populist anger in America and the EU widens, it is not difficult to imagine politicians channeling people's frustrations away from those on the other side of the aisle toward those on the other side of the ocean. In the near future, American policy might look to remedy long-standing grievances with China's trade practices through political actions. China could respond by limiting access to its domestic markets. In recent history we have yet to see the American political system put forward a successful national candidate or an ideology that governs by forcing tough choices. The path of least resistance is taken every time. With respect to China, this political cowardice is bad news. Given America's recent politics, the most likely outcome of an increasingly tense relationship between the United States and China suggests the disastrous option will be the one we pursue. Relative to U.S.-China relations, the easy path will be one of escalation and recrimination. Given America's current economic insecurities, to which we will next turn, this path is becoming more and more likely.

5

America's Economic Insecurity

"My greatest fear, though, is that Americans will be inclined to blame China for a wide range of the economic problems we face at home.... If we adopt such an attitude, it will divert us from addressing the changes we need to make at home."

—Robert D. Hormats, interview with *Asia Society*, March 5, 2012

From the comfort of my office in Seattle, it is easy to forget that a big part of America is hurting. In the aftermath of the 2016 election, progressives were awash in equal parts introspection, self-loathing, and grumbling about a part of the country many here on the West Coast do not understand. But I do. I was born in Plymouth, Indiana, where early on my family lived in a mobile home park across from Centennial Park, not too far away from the little hospital where I was born. I grew up and spent most of my childhood in small towns in northern Indiana. A good number of my family are blue-collar people who historically were proud Democrats but who have over the last twenty years become more and more conservative. The kids I went to school with had parents who worked in factories, drove school buses, worked as waitstaff at local restaurants, and all in all, were hardworking folks who did not have a lot. I married a farmer's daughter from one of the most industrious and decent families you would ever want to know. Since leaving northern Indiana, my wife and I have lived in Boston, Nashville, Indianapolis, and now Seattle, which is to say that accidentally we have accumulated a set of life experiences that merges together our more rural upbringing with our more urban adult lives.

Moving away from where we were both raised is equal parts good and bad. It's bad because of the difficulty staying engaged with family and friends; good because of the opportunities, both personal and professional, we have been able to pursue. However, when we reflect on where we come from and what has changed since we left, one common thread emerges: how economically anxious the folks we grew up with are. To be more specific, they all seem to share a pervasive sense that they are working just as hard as their parents did (and in many cases harder), only to fall further and further behind, more and more into debt they fear they will never be able to pay off. This economic anxiety is rarely expressed directly; rather, friends and family tend to focus on leaders, both in politics and business, who seem unable to appreciate that a healthy economy requires actual intentional choices to benefit the middle class. Want to understand what happened in the 2016 presidential election? As with any big historical inflection point, the reasons are many. But front and center are people's economic anxieties, and for good reason.

In the period immediately following World War II, every near-peer economic power that the United States now competes with economically was destroyed. Germany, Japan, China, all gone. The economic might the United States assembled and the benefits that accrued to our middle class in the years after this era were aberrations. They were historical anomalies. Economically, victory in World War II left the United States the unassailable strongman. Our manufacturing output amounted to more than half of the world's total. Let that sink in: more than half of anything that was manufactured anywhere in the world was made here. No surprise that this period is thought of as the golden era for a middle-class worker who did not have to go to college. When your economic competition is literally in rubble, you win simply by having capacity.

The middle class that America remembers today was the result of a historically unique tragedy in World War II. Most importantly, if the United States wanted to maintain the integrity of its middle class, it would have approached globalization and the means by which we invest in education, infrastructure, and innovation with much more attention, discipline, and focus than we did. If politicians and policy makers in the United States had worked as hard as their counterparts in Germany, Japan, and China did in the decades after World War II, much of the economic insecurity we feel today could have been mitigated.

This is not to suggest economic pressures on the middle class would have gone away; rather, most Americans would be better off and better educated, and would have a more elastic political system capable of thoughtful policy making. This reinforces a profound point: it is the conceptualization and coordination of a society's response to these pressures that constitutes good government. When government cannot help its citizens navigate these moments, people turn to those who promise to burn that government to the ground. After all, if government cannot help, then what is the point tolerating all its intrusions and excesses?

This same period laid the groundwork for many American multinationals that dominate the world's economy today. Beyond economic gains, the American culture, way of life, and political ideas were elevated to global ideals—standards they richly deserved. American politics put forward a vision that government was empowered by the consent of its citizens, that personal freedom was an absolute necessity, and that this freedom was integral to economic growth. American movies exported a vision of what it was like to live in America, admittedly with Hollywood's own spin. American-made products embodied the best version someone in the middle class anywhere around the world would ever aspire to own and enjoy.

Among the questions that should keep policy makers awake at night is where America's pooled economic anxiety will be directed. Trump is only the beginning. Make no mistake: there are worse demagogues than Trump, and they will happily offer the cheapest solutions to the most expensive problems our country faces. Building walls, tearing up trade agreements, pulling out of defense treaties, these are all minor compared to what additional economic pain could make politically viable. Deeper, uglier, and more irreversible impulses are at work, ones that will only get worse if the Trump administration fails to improve the lives of those who most need positive disruptive change. Right now most of this anger is being directed at DC. But that is going to dissipate as people begin to recognize that the capital is built to encourage stalemates, to inhibit radical change, and to protect the status quo. Where will all of the resulting anger and frustration go? Perhaps it will be directed toward the 1 percent, if an American political party can ever dislodge the uniquely American idea that people are poor somehow because they deserve to be and that society's inequalities are a necessary precondition for a healthy version of capitalism. Perhaps the anxiety will be directed at technologists and the companies who profit from automating people's jobs. But try being angry at a robot. It is nowhere near as satisfying as being angry at another country. The single most satisfying vessel to contain America's rage and channel our collective economic insecurity will not be technology; it will be a country, a race, a part of the world a long way away, whose differences beg to become caricatures of our own misplaced anger.

When American policy makers fully embraced globalization, the country was economically secure. The years immediately after the collapse of the Soviet Union and the end of the Cold War elevated the Washington model to a position of unquestioned primacy. No one dared assert an alternative way to manage an economy or political system: the Washington Consensus was dominant. In this moment, America adopted a generous position toward the world as a whole and toward China specifically. After all, no one questioned that this period was—as Francis Fukuyama famously put it—the "end of history." Ideas about globalization were deeply encoded within the belief that no country could forever resist American ideals. The end of the Cold War was understood to be the most recent expression of essential insights that flowed all the way from the European Enlightenment and that had now been perfectly expressed in America's victory of the Soviet Union. As grand as China's own three-millennia history might be, it was no match for all that Western society had learned about how government and the individual were to relate to one another. No matter how entrenched another country's system of governance was in an opposing ideology, its government would ultimately have to look more or less like America's—which is to say, with an empowered individual able to direct government policy through the expression of his opinion and vote in a democracy. Any other form of government would ultimately be unable to harness civilization's powers of innovation and success. Consequently, no matter what a country's founding ideology might be, it would ultimately bend toward a version that looked like America.

Supporting ideas about how America would handle potentially harmful economic dislocations during this process of globalization were trivialized. Progressives emphasized the role of new high-technology jobs and the service industries as ways to support any short-term economic pain. Pro-business conservatives, in an embrace of free market fundamentalism, confidently asserted that the invisible hand of the free market would see labor geographically and vocationally reorganize. Both approaches badly missed the mark on how globalization would impact Middle America. While trade with China definitely created many benefits, it also coincided with an era of economic insecurity for America's middle class. This moment was not purely China's—or globalization's—fault. Rather, the economic insecurity of the American middle class today reflects long-standing unaddressed issues around rising costs of health care, housing, education, and childcare.

Today, China's economic success stands in stark contrast to how America feels about itself. In particular, where China has a national industrial and economic policy, America does not, and now our political dysfunction prevents us from having one. Where China has spent the last several decades mobilizing its labor force and investing in massive infrastructure projects, the United States' most coordinated policies have been to ensure a low cost of capital so our McMansion-building spree could continue. Missed opportunities in America around our crumbling infrastructure abound, as does a lack of political will to tackle big domestic problems around health care, vocational training programs, and the costs of education and childcare.

Since the aftermath of the 2008 financial crisis, when the American government chose to intervene and support companies like GM, Chrysler, AIG, and the largest of the nation's banks, public mood has soured on the role of government in the nation's economy. The American government decided to stabilize a situation they believed could spiral out of control and take the entire financial system down with it. While in hindsight many conservative politicians in particular have rejected this idea, the belief among members of both parties who were in the middle of the crisis was that we were on the threshold of another Great Depression. Many conservatives in government at the time understood this and, behind closed doors, acknowledged government had to act as an external stabilizer for the market's momentary lack of rationality. The best version of conservative economics has always been to point out that for government to be able to act as a stabilizer in this sort of situation, it needs to have its finances in order once a crisis presents itself. Until recently, it has never been the position of thoughtful conservatives that a crisis should lead to structural systemic failures across American commerce when the companies themselves were perfectly healthy but for a moment of force majeure. As most Americans understand, you should save up for a rainy day, but when that day comes, you should pry open the piggy bank.

Heading into the 2008 financial crisis, the American government did not have a strong balance sheet. Long-term entitlement programs were on unsustainable spending curves, while wars in Iraq and Afghanistan, Bush-era tax cuts, and the Bush-era prescription drug plan all were unfunded. Whether these were good or bad policies are beside the point for now. The twin issues heading into 2008 were that the American government's financial condition was not good, and Americans broadly distrusted their elected leaders to make the necessary choices to reposition the country's economy in the face of globalization's unrelenting pressure. Because of the political gamesmanship of the moments after the 2008 financial crisis through the budget showdowns that become a nearly annual occurrence during the Obama presidency, American cynicism toward what good the government could do is at an all-time high, which is why an economically insecure populace would turn toward someone like Donald Trump to disrupt a system they see as unresponsive to their concerns. But this is not all. Donald Trump only becomes an option when people stop believing that government actually matters; it is no coincidence that his presidency took the path of Republican politics. After all, it has been Republicans who for years set up a laugh track about government, channeling Ronald Reagan's quote that "the nine most terrifying words in the English language are, 'I'm from the government and I'm here to help.'" If government does not matter, in fact if government is actually a constraint on society achieving fairness, equality, peace, and justice, then why not send a buffoon to run it? And progressives, in a stunning failure to recognize the danger inherent within this world view, refused to acknowledge the need for government to be particularly careful and competent in the post–Cold War era and left open the door for precisely this moment of brinksmanship. After all, when the people who are actually in government cannot run it effectively, from the point of view of an average voter, what stood to be lost in handing the government over to someone entirely new to governing? Even better is someone who claims to be on their side and out to rid DC of those special interests that only serve the 1 percent.

Our political environment has turned so harshly against the idea of an interventionist government that it is almost impossible to advocate for the idea of the government's hand in our national industrial policy. This attitude is a cancer in American thinking and one that our Chinese counterparts do not understand or share. Instead of asking whether government has made the right choices in the policies it has pursued, Americans are asking whether government has any role to play at all. Where our economic competitors, not just in China but also in Europe and the Asia-Pacific, ask *how much* and *where* to spend government funds to best incentivize research and development, America asks *whether* and *if*. Gone is the ability to talk rationally about whether we have prioritized the right programs and whether government can act constructively to advance American competitiveness, domestic industry, and the American middle class. We have turned so severely against the idea of competent government that we may have set in motion the sort of populist rage against our own government that history warns us always ends badly. America's economic insecurity has sown the seeds for domestic anarchy that only a strongman will be able to control.

AMERICA DOESN'T REALLY HAVE A PLAN

Within the United States' broader economic anxiety are several more specific concerns, the first of which is that Americans suspect the country's leaders do not have a plan for how to move the domestic economy forward in the twenty-first century. Elites roll their eyes at how "obvious" it is that protectionism does not work, that it does nothing to benefit the American worker and might actually make things worse, and yet from the point of view of the American worker, what is the answer to the economic anxieties of America's middle class? Protectionism might be wrong, but from the perspective of the average person, it quickly becomes something actionable. Donald Trump won the 2016 election for a number of reasons, but one was that he was willing to say out loud what a lot of disgruntled Americans had been feeling for some time: "the status quo isn't working for me, my leaders don't care about me, and they don't have a plan to make my life better." In such a moment, tearing down the established order makes a lot of sense.

American fears about China are actually frustrations about how America's political leaders have failed to craft a coherent vision for America's economic future. Whatever gripes we may have with China's leadership, no government in recent history has been as effective as China's has been at lifting its people out of poverty. If we were to take China's economic metrics and project them onto a country or region we do not feel threatened by—say, Africa—we would applaud that country's success on both ideological and humanitarian grounds. We would hold them up as the example by which other poverty-stricken countries should learn; we would call it a great good, rush to study it, and make it an object lesson for those in need. For the briefest of periods, China's rise was greeted along similar lines. Now that its success has diverged from our own, deep insecurities have presented themselves related to our future, leadership, and foundational ideas about the role of government.

Among the carryovers from China's collectivist past is its ability to think and execute more as a group than is common in Western culture, something that runs contrary to what Americans believe has been essential to our success: radical individualism. Under Mao, this was a disastrous competency that made the joke about lemmings going off a cliff all too accurate. Under Deng and Chinese leaders since, it has proven to be an extremely effective characteristic. Where Mao arbitrarily set industrial production targets and then forced the Chinese people to find a way to make it happen, China's current leadership focuses on key industries. It sets in motion strategies that entail domestic investment, targeted openness to foreigners in pursuit of new technology, and dedicated institutional support to ensure that the country and its businesses achieve the goals of the party's Five-Year Plans (5YPs). Many of these plans have resulted in excess capacity that will ultimately be a problem. America's westward expansion and investment in rail capacity after our own Civil War followed a similar trajectory: expansion, overinvestment, crash, capacity rationalization, and growth. Countries that experience high growth tend to overinvest because they have the money to do so and because the inputs (labor and materials specifically) are cheap.

Once the object of ridicule, 5YPs are something China watchers have learned to pay attention to. While China may come up short of the goals these plans establish, it has been more common that the plans meet, and in some cases, overachieve their objectives. Recent 5YPs have emphasized China's need to continue to build infrastructure; secure the necessary raw materials and energy supplies that will support its economic growth; shrink its income disparities; transition the national economy built on low-wage, high-labor content manufacturing to high-wage, high-technology innovative products and services. Not all of the objectives of China's 5YPs are defined so generally: in some cases, the country announces its strategy for specific industries. Examples of this have included cars and TVs and, more recently, cleantech, biotech and commercial aviation. As China's economy has prospered, achieving these goals has become more difficult because the new industries the plans have begun to target are more sophisticated and technically challenging. Regardless, the world has noted that the country's leadership is more often successful than not at achieving them.

Meeting these 5YPs is possible in some ways because China's politics take a back seat toward achieving their economic goals. Critics of China are quick to point out that these 5YPs are pursued with such vigor because their success allows the party to stay in power. However, if creating positive economic outcomes for its people as a means for holding onto power is bad, then what else should China's leaders be focused on? While we may dislike and disagree with many of the other policies designed to ensure the party maintains control, America would be better off if both Democrats and Republicans viewed their ability to create positive economic opportunities for the average American as a source of their political fortunes. Say what we may about China's politics, one of its orienting ideas is that the politicians only get to stay in power if the economy is growing.

At the same time Chinese politics have been single-minded in their fixation around the country's economy, American politics has made triangulation over a handful of divisive social issues the means by which elections are determined. This is why once-senator and former GOP presidential candidate Rick Santorum can say to potential caucus voters in Iowa that only when we ban gay marriage will our economy get back on track.[1] Political discourse, no stranger to red-baiting and red herrings, has degenerated to levels not seen since America's own Civil War. In contrast, China's politics is primarily focused on developing an economic strategy. Is it any wonder China is beating us at our own game when they maintain such a high-level focus on how best to grow their economy?

Practically, part of why China is able to work in this way is how they have structured their most important political events. China's 5YP and their People's Congress both occur on five-year cycles, with the highest offices in the lands changing hands even less frequently. Among other inherent advantages over the American processes are that the longer the horizon, the more time is allowed for political fights to break out, be resolved, and actual progress toward policy objectives to occur. The American electoral process now runs in what are effectively not even two-year cycles. During these two years, American congressmen find the majority of their time is spent placating special interests who have the available funds that will allow them to run again. The net of this is that congressmen come into office only to get ready to run again, with only the slightest time to focus on complex issues like how to best compete against China or what the role of Washington should be in developing an industrial policy. No wonder blind political orthodoxy now substitutes for pragmatic policy making on what actually works to create economic opportunity for American families.

Whatever critics might think about China's political process, it maximizes the opportunity for government planners to strategize, implement, and measure outcomes. None of this is to suggest that China's model is perfect. There are many reasons to be suspicious of the idea that China's model is fundamentally better than ours. But what they are doing better today is focusing their limited resources on a plan they all agree has the best chance to lift their people out of poverty and create a middle class. Americans would do well to ask of our leaders the same discipline and focus.

AMERICA'S POOR ALIGNMENT OF RESOURCES

Why can China achieve these goals and we cannot? Why is China taking the lead in cleantech sectors and in high-speed rail, while we are following? If the United States cannot lead the way in the development, manufacturing, and sale of high-value goods like these, then what hope do we have of competing with China in any sector of the global economy? China owes its success in areas like cleantech to two things: First, in many cases they have put more resources into these sectors than we have. Second, in China the government makes it easy for new and therefore unproven high-technology businesses to build their pilot plants faster and with fewer regulatory roadblocks. Beyond enormous amounts of capital and keeping the regulatory regime streamlined, China's government looks to create as many incentives as it can to allow nascent industries to take root first in China. These incentives include cheap land, tax incentives, low interest loans from government-owned banks, and investment in infrastructure that will ultimately support cleantech facilities. In a recent cleantech meeting I attended in the United States, the American businessmen in attendance bemoaned the reality that their best chance of raising the most capital the quickest and getting their pilot plant running the fastest was if they went to China. With all this speed comes mistakes, some of which China may soon regret. But for this industry in particular, China's lack of regulatory challenges makes it easy to carve out a leadership position in cleantech.

Simply put, once China establishes as part of its national economy strategy that a sector like wind power is a national priority, it aligns resources to ensure that industry achieves its stated goals. What has happened in clean-technology could happen in other high-technology parts of the American economy, which would only add more to the economic anxieties here.

The American government has tried to do some of these same things, but is always handcuffed by political orthodoxy and a "gotcha" form of politics that prevents domestic politicians from taking any real risks. In addition, America's recent emphasis on limited government means we believe government should not be picking technologies or industries for investment. While the Chinese talk about what government should be doing (which technologies to prioritize—coal versus wind, solar versus nuclear), we talk about whether government should be doing anything at all. We believe the market will signal to entrepreneurs that it needs alternatives to conventional sources of energy and that the market will then distribute scarce capital to unproven technologies with the hope that they will become proven and ultimately profitable businesses. The American model is built on the idea that venture capitalists will evaluate new technologies, choose to invest in them, and wait three to five years for an exit opportunity (usually selling their company to an established firm or an initial public offering [IPO]).

At least three problems with this model have emerged in the last decade: First, the equity markets have to be robust to support this sort of exit. If the market tanks as it did after the 2008 financial crisis, the exit for these investors evaporates. Many are reluctant to make investments exactly in moments like that, when they are most needed. The second problem with this model is that no matter the wealth of this select group of people, they will never match the government's capacity to invest. Consequently, America is working with smart but extremely finite capital from highly motivated venture capitalists, against less sophisticated but much larger amounts of capital from just as highly motivated government planners in Beijing. Third, it remains to be seen whether the venture capitalist model is capable of producing the sort of financing for early-stage bench science that government has traditionally funded.

Because the time horizon for most venture capitalist investments is typically shorter than that of government investments, they tend to emphasize existing science that is transitioning into practical engineering and applied technology. This is a critical distinction: without a strong pipeline of core research science, the venture capital model runs dry. The Chinese model, for good and bad, is more aggressive with the state's money. Some of this is not insight by China into the inadequacies of the venture capital model; rather, it is an accidental overhang from China's planned economy and the ongoing role of the central government in making investments into what they believe is best.

The role of government that conservatives have traditionally supported has been for government to incentivize science. Much of this investment will result only in academic outcomes, but some will enrich the nation's productive scientific ecosystem, spurring a wave of opportunities that venture capital and industry can access. Because we are not making enough of these investments now, we are laying the groundwork for downside risks to America's economic future that could be much worse than they need to be, purely because of domestic politics. A good example of this are the last several presidential administrations' funding of the National Institutes of Health (NIH). According to the Federation of American Societies for Experimental Biology, "from FY 2003 to 2015, the National Institutes of Health (NIH) lost 22% of its capacity to fund research due to budget cuts, sequestration, and inflationary losses."[2]

While the 2016 NIH budget from the Obama administration reversed this trend with a 5.9 percent funding increase, current inflation-adjusted spending on the NIH is still well below its 2003 level. Among the sectors where the United States should be leading, biotech must be at or near the top. The unique ecosystem required to incubate biotechnology companies has rarely been replicated outside of the United States. Because of America's unique efforts in this space, the biotechnology community employs over eight hundred thousand people directly and supports 3.4 million jobs in the United States. These jobs are the direct result of decades of investment, partnerships, and shared risk between the American government, academia, venture capital, and biotechnology companies. The net of these investments has been the ecosystem that China very much wants to recreate in order to compete with American biotechnology companies.

American policy makers tend to assume this ecosystem is self-sustaining when it is no such thing. Biotech will require similar tending to through coordinated government policy in the United States, much like as its counterpart is receiving at the hands of the Chinese government. This is the sort of mistake American policy makes which China does not: we are so focused on market mechanisms that we are unwilling to admit the good that comes from government's investment in key research. Government investments need to be financially justifiable and with a clearly delineated hierarchy of priorities, but to turn our back on the positive contributions government can make toward leading a competitive response to China is shortsighted and will only make American economic anxieties worse.

BALANCING PROTECTIONISM AND FREE MARKET FUNDAMENTALISM

Nothing shines a light more brightly on people's stance on China than introducing the idea of protectionism. Advocates of free trade believe the world is better when nations compete with the fewest impediments. In this definition the words "world" and "nations" figure prominently, and for good reason. As critics of free trade point out, while the effect of free trade at the global level might very well be to increase the standard of living for impoverished countries, the effect at the national level for more developed economies is not always as positive. To critics this is because the economic dislocation experienced by workers in developed economies who see their jobs migrate to lower-cost locales like China and Mexico is more severe than advocates of free trade are willing to acknowledge.

Two well-known advocates of free trade, Tom Friedman and Paul Krugman, both come from liberal political backgrounds. This is fascinating as it shows the extent the traditionally liberal establishment, long a bastion of strength for organized labor, embraced the idea of free trade during the nineties. Friedman's and Krugman's advocacy owes much to their belief that nothing improves people's lives more than economic well-being. In the heady days of 1997, Krugman wrote a now-infamous column for *Slate* titled, "In Praise of Cheap Labor: Bad jobs at bad wages are better than no jobs at all."[3] Read now, Krugman's column seems almost quaint in its faith that American workers would not be harmed as globalization advanced.

Krugman writes, "the lofty moral tone of the opponents of globalization is possible only because they have chosen not to think their position through. While fat-cat capitalists might benefit from globalization, the biggest beneficiaries are, yes, Third World workers." On this limited point, he is correct. The challenge when he wrote this was to make sure that the workers displaced in the United States had opportunities to move into other industries. During this period, our focus was elsewhere. We believed that high-technology industries would displace American factories, making the American middle-class blue-collar laborer a relic of the past. How exactly these workers would move into new sectors of the economy was poorly considered.

Friedman, whose most famous book *The World Is Flat* added to the American vocabulary the idea of the "flat world," is someone whose works deserve rereading now. While he is certainly a similar advocate for free trade as Krugman, Friedman's books have an edge to them that people likely missed when *The World Is Flat* was first published. Reading his classic in the midst of our current economic anxieties is a different experience than reading it at the height of the dot-com bubble or in the pre-9/11 days when America was more confident about its place in the world. It is all too easy to read about the global markets he presents, in the flat world where, as he put it, no two countries who both had McDonald's had ever gone to war against each other, and think of all the upside potential, but Friedman wanted his readers to take away something more. There were also downside risks he pointed toward.

The World Is Flat asks readers to think about how America is going to compete against these increasingly industrious, highly focused, and hungry countries. As Friedman wrote, "the great challenge for our time will be to absorb these changes in ways that do not overwhelm people but also do not leave them behind."[4] What many now admit is that his warnings were not heeded. The changes have not only overwhelmed people, leaving them behind, they have also resulted in people feeling angry at a world they neither understand nor feel ready to compete in.

In his more recent writing, Friedman has turned much of his attention away from the international stage to the national, focusing on the problems he sees within the United States. As Friedman sees it, America's lack of political fortitude suggests our nation will continue to struggle to meet the challenges of the twenty-first century. In one such column, Friedman reflected on how the challenges of his childhood were different from those of his children's: "Everyone is going to have to run a little faster to advance his or her standard of living. When I was growing up, my parents used to say to me, 'Tom, finish your dinner—people in China are starving.' I am now telling my own daughters, 'Girls, finish your homework—people in China and India are starving for your jobs.'"[5] Should American politics make substantive changes impossible or should people in the United States decide the personal changes required of them are simply too much, America will likely go down the path of protectionism. This will always be the more obvious and certainly easier choice. It also has the potential to be a dangerous decision. One of the choices made by the worlds' governments in the thirties that made the Great Depression longer and more severe than necessary was protectionist measures introduced around the globe, the most well-known example of which was the American Smoot-Hawley Act.

Has our attitude toward free trade been too generous? Have we taken such a liberal attitude toward open markets that we have looked beyond the understandable if limited role the government should play balancing between openness and protection? While there is a fine line to walk between protectionism and free trade, we have embraced free trade with too little attention paid toward the impact free trade policies would have on the American worker. In addition, American policy toward China erred when it did not single-mindedly focus our limited resources on ways to ensure dislocated workers were retrained for new industries and that new industries had every incentive government could throw their way to get them from the conceptual to job-creating stages. Admittedly, a more gradual approach to trade with China would have encountered resistance from American multinational companies who understood the enormous cost advantages possible if they could relocate their manufacturing facilities to China. This is where a strong government in Washington actively looking to balance the needs of workers with the opportunities for business would have been able to both encourage these companies' expansion into China and urge them to give the American economy the time and resources to ensure an orderly transition. In countries like Japan, Germany, and South Korea, native multinational companies feel a depth of allegiance to their nation that is not easily severed from their company's identity. They manage also to be aggressive global competitors who participate in globalization, a fine line our own corporate and governmental policies should be able to walk.

Clyde Prestowitz, the Reagan administration counselor to the secretary of commerce, vice chairman of the Clinton administration Commission on Trade and Investment in the Asia-Pacific Region, and member of the advisory board of the U.S. Export-Import Bank, wrote of what he saw as a certain naïvete from DC politicians about encouraging American multinational companies to do a better job of managing their responsibilities to the United States:

> In 2011, GE CEO Jeff Immelt was chairman of President Obama's Council on Jobs and Competitiveness. At the same time, GE announced that it was entering into a joint venture with China's state-owned Aviation Industry Corporation (AVIC) to transfer much of its avionics production and development to China. "What?" Obama must have said. Avionics is what all the economic theories say America should be involved in—it's high tech, and it's not labor intensive. For trade negotiators, however, the decision was not surprising. China has made aviation a target industry for the future. It also has a large market for aircraft. GE wants to sell avionics to that market. So China is telling GE that if it wants the sale it will have to produce in China and transfer jobs and technology there. Of course, no one says it that directly. But that's the game. It would be interesting to know if Immelt called Obama before making the announcement, or if Obama called him afterward.[6]

In fairness to China and proponents of unfettered free trade, it is worth recalling that many of these industries were led to believe they were not welcome in certain communities. Many were told the sort of jobs they had to offer were not those that Americans in the twenty-first century would want. It is perfectly understandable that American industry and China's leadership are now confused about American frustrations. After all, China has been the recipient of jobs we told them we really did not want; now, in a moment of economic desperation, we want them back. Blame China for our lost jobs if you will but only after admitting that many of these jobs were ones we said we did not want in the first place and willingly gave them.

China has less of a problem walking the line between the free market and protectionism. In the midst of their policy response to the 2008 financial crisis, Beijing put together a $586 billion stimulus plan. Specifically designed to address concerns the party had that the recession in the West might spread to China, many protectionist measures were included in the Chinese stimulus. Within the plan were requirements that money be spent only on domestically produced goods, a criterion that walled off much of the government's lucrative spending on infrastructure. China made sure as much of its stimulus money went to benefit its own companies as possible, an example of how China plays the globalization game.

What is America to do about this? Can we afford at this late stage to enable protectionist thinking as a reasonable response to China? Many in the policy community worry it is too late: no sense trying to put the toothpaste back in the tube. The larger question this poses is what Dani Rodrik wrote about in his book *The Globalization Paradox*. In it, Rodrik develops the idea of shallow versus deep globalization. Shallow globalization is how China participates in world trade: it goes along only so far as is absolutely necessary, but no further. A good example of this is China's stance on what is known as the Agreement on Government Procurement portion of the WTO protocols. China has chosen to not comply with the regulations of that agreement. By doing this, China protected a large portion of its economy from foreign competition. It acts to protect its domestic companies and to give the attainment of national economic goals primacy over international standards of accountability or free trade. This is in contrast to how the United States and the European Union practice globalization, which is what Rodrik calls "deep globalization." Here countries go much further in an attempt to embody and empower globalization, many times to the detriment of their citizens, because they believe in the innate good created by a deep and enriched form of globalization.

Balancing between these two extremes is not easy, and it should surprise no one that American policy now is beginning to pursue a shallower version of globalization, both in terms of policies it advocates for, as well as practices it chooses to reward American businesses for. Proponents of deep globalization have to answer this question: if the United States proves unable to jump-start its economy and create wins for its middle class, then is not the resulting unsettled, insecure, and fragile America a long-term threat to globalization? Might a more gradual and shallower globalization have made sense? Since the early nineties, American policy could afford to be unusually generous in the policies it advocated for and put into place relative to shallow versus deep globalization. The unfortunate reality that advocates of deep globalization will soon have to acknowledge is that American government in particular wasted the years in between the 1990s and the 2010s. This has left the national economy in fragile condition, with a working class that needs some special attention to prevent their pent-up frustrations from being unleashed on China.

AMERICA'S MISSED OPPORTUNITIES

In the United States the first day of school brings with it many traditions: the new backpack, the squeaky gym shoes, and the awkward glances around in an attempt to find familiar faces and size up the unfamiliar ones. One of the most common traditions was, I now suspect, also one of our teachers' favorites (it did make planning that first awkward day of class much easier): telling the class how you spent your summer. Americans now need a similar and no less awkward show-and-tell moment, but this time instead of "how I spent my summer," it would be "how I spent the nineties." How America used its time, energy, and resources during this period says everything about why our country is now struggling.

During the nineties America's public policy pursued and our cultural values largely reflected four myths: the myth of easy credit, the myth of homes as our best investment, the myth that a services economy could supplant a manufacturing economy (a version of which is the myth that high-technology manufacturing could displace heavy industry), and the myth that economic growth for the developing world would offset the economic dislocation of the American middle class. These four myths were self-perpetuated. China played a role as these myths became part of American values, but they were ideas we designed and pursued of our own volition.

As many of the most pervasive myths tend to be, these myths were true for a time. Both easy credit and perpetually higher prices for American homes were, from the late nineties to the 2008 financial crisis, the norm. American consumers were encouraged to view credit as something beneficial, debt a tool money savvy people should use to their advantage. Underneath the helpful ways credit can expand an economy were troubling indicators that credit had become a crutch: the percentage of disposable household income that went toward debt payments hit an all-time high in the second half of 2007, and during that same period American household savings dipped below 1 percent.

For many Dragon Slayers, who also tend to be fiscally conservative, these were ominous signs that people were looking past the likely economic dislocation and pain that China's rise would lead to. Americans had fallen into the trap of believing that cheap money made taking on debt forever manageable. A handful of analysts have put forward the idea that the recent era of cheap credit, of which Americans happily partook, was a result of China's one-sided currency policy that benefits their export economy while accumulating vast quantities of U.S. dollars. In this way, they argue, China is actually responsible for the debt servitude of America's middle class.

During the nineties, seemingly ever-increasing 401k values coupled with rising real estate prices led many to believe the increase in their asset values would offset any increase in debt payments. Easy credit made it difficult for most Americans to recognize that their personal income was not rising. A study conducted by Ethan Pollack at the EPI Policy Center showed that "between 2001 and 2007, the real income of the median working-age household decreased by 1.9%, a loss of $1,107, despite productivity increasing by 18% over that time."[7] No small surprise that the 2016 election was marked by angry middle-class Americans who felt they had been working harder and falling further behind, and all the while big faceless companies and China were benefiting at their expense.

What about college-educated workers? After all, they were supposed to be the group that benefited the most from globalization and the "new economy." According to Pollack, "wages for workers with a college degree increased by just 0.4% between 2001 and 2007." Annalyn Censky at CNN *Money* wrote in February of 2011 that "incomes for 90% of Americans have been stuck in neutral, and it's not just because of the Great Recession. Middle-class incomes have been stagnant for at least a generation."[8] She goes on to write, "in 1988, the income of an average American taxpayer was $33,400, adjusted for inflation. Fast forward 20 years, and not much had changed: The average income was still just $33,000 in 2008, according to IRS data."[9] American consumers were beginning to grow suspicious: all this globalization had definitely been good for China, and it had certainly led to Wal-Mart and GE doing well, but when it came time to look at their own personal financial situation and job security, things felt worse than ever.

Nowhere was cheap credit more destructive than in the mythology it enabled in the U.S. housing market. Many now suspect that if American policy had been as attuned to the needs of the manufacturing sector as it was to the housing sector, more blue-collar workers would have held onto their jobs. Washington, long predisposed toward the idea of homeownership as a great good, pushed for policies that would make homeownership the norm. To make this happen required not just cheap credit but also encouraging banks to lend into parts of the market that previously did not have access to reliable credit. Questions about the prudence of this policy approach were quickly pushed aside by both Democrats and Republicans. After all, which politician really wants to argue against the uniquely American ideal of a house surrounded by a white picket fence? While this was happening, America's trade unions grumbled to themselves about how much better off the American manufacturing sector would be if it received the same focused energy as China's was.

The third myth, that a service economy would supplant a manufacturing economy, was common during the debates around extending most favored nation status to China as well as the push for the North American Free Trade Association. Dragon Slayers loudly protested this myth and have held firm to the belief that the transition from manufacturing to service jobs was never going to be as clean as free market fundamentalists would have had the public believe. Too few in DC pushed back against how demoralizing and destabilizing losing manufacturing jobs would be. Ohio congressman Tim Ryan acidly gave voice to these concerns when he said, "some of our workers, literally, their last act at the factory was to unbolt the machines and load them up to be shipped to China."[10] Americans had convinced themselves that the transition from a manufacturing-intensive economy to a services economy would create enough new jobs that the net effect to blue-collar American workers would be minimal. Many from organized labor never believed this. Yet back in the go-go nineties, America seemed all too happy to get rid of many manufacturing jobs.

In the nineties unemployment became a chronic problem for America but not like today; then, there were too few workers available for hire. Unemployment bottomed out at 3.7 percent, a level that most economists believe is below what is healthy for an economy. Beneath this percentage, wage inflation is highly probable. Consequently, it did not seem too much of a leap of faith to suggest that America could afford to—and probably needed to—ship some manufacturing jobs overseas. Because avoiding inflation was, after the high inflation of the seventies, the central pursuit of government monetary policy, actions to cool the American labor market seemed sensible. Want those manufacturing jobs we sent to China back? It is hard to blame the Chinese for being confused over our changing attitude when we were the ones who asked to ship them off in the first place.

A particular version of this myth was even more troubling: that a high-technology manufacturing economy could replace a low-technology-heavy industry. No better example of this exists than Apple products. Many adore the combination of sophisticated design, simple engineering, streamlined logistics, and great customer service that have defined my experience with their products. While the Apple model is a great example of American innovation and ingenuity, it also could have been a great example of the American manufacturing jobs that could have been created as a result of these products being sold to consumers around the world. They are high-technology products that require sophisticated capital equipment and well-trained workers to deliver quality products at reasonable prices. So why are each of these Apple products made overseas and not in America? Industry analysts believe labor accounts for roughly 7 percent of the cost of a finished iPhone; even if American labor was twice that, the offset by having higher quality American labor doing the work should have been a compelling argument for these jobs to stay in the United States. Why is Apple not pushing for parts of their supply chain—admittedly the higher-end products—to come from America?

Even if Apple wanted to make their products domestically, they would not be able to. According to Steve Jobs's authorized biographer Walter Isaacson, this was a point Jobs made to President Obama. The industries Apple needs are not in the United States anymore, and in some cases never were. Countries like Taiwan, South Korea, and Japan moved aggressively through government-sponsored initiatives to build skills and create enormous incentives around specific industries they believed would be key to the future. It may be anathema to say this given American's current loathing of anything government sponsored—but the Asian countries that now manufacture the iPhone and iPad many years ago allowed their governments to play an active role creating an ecosystem for these manufacturers. We could have done the same thing, but our prosperity blinded us to the ways these countries were positioning their economies. In addition, our political allegiance to the idea that the state has no role to play in helping early-stage industries build a domestic foundation was disastrously shortsighted.

Writing in a 2009 issue of *Harvard Business Review*, Gary Pisano and Willy Shih made note of what they called "A Sign of Trouble" in their article "Restoring American Competitiveness." They write that going back to 2000, America's trade balance specific to high-technology products had begun to decrease and that by 2002 "it turned negative for the first time and continued to decline through 2007."[11] If Dragon Slayers were right, China would become a competitor in every sector of American industry—both low and high tech—more rapidly than the American worker would be able to respond, which would further intensify the economic pressures middle-class America would have to face. As anyone in IT, biotech, or advanced manufacturing will be quick say, this is precisely what has happened. China's high-technology capabilities have evolved much more rapidly than many expected. The family member with a PhD in biology who thought she had a safe and secure job in biotech now realizes she will have to compete with a Chinese bench scientist in Hangzhou, with the same pressure on wages and work hours that blue-collar American workers have already faced. Want to know when conflict with China is nearly inevitable? When an unscrupulous politician can say the same negative thing about China to a PhD and a welder and have them both believe that China is the cause of their shared anxieties.

During the mid-nineties in particular, we defined to China what the terms of trade between our two countries were going to be: we would ship them low-value, high-labor manufacturing jobs, and they would use these to advance their economy by exporting back to the United States. China was following our lead; we were the masters, and they were the pupils. We had convinced ourselves that the transition from a manufacturing-intensive economy to a services economy would create enough new jobs that the net effect to blue-collar American workers would be minimal. It is not China's fault that we now wish we had proceeded more slowly any more than it is the fault of the American worker for being more expensive than his counterpart in Wuxi.

One of the world's leading experts on the role government can play to help drive industrial innovation is Dan Breznitz, a professor at the University of Toronto. His book *Innovation and the State* uses three examples of countries that have built systems enabling their governments to play active roles in driving innovation. The countries are Israel, Taiwan, and Ireland. Against the backdrop of a political environment in America that has made it impossible to argue for the good government can do in promoting certain industries, Breznitz's conclusions are worth quoting at length:

> First, the state needs to actively engage with industry to solve the fundamental market failure in industrial R&D. Otherwise, the inherent characteristics of industrial R&D—its indivisibility, inappropriability,

and high uncertainties, all of which are accentuated in the case of emerging economies with their lack of technological capabilities and finance—would lead private investors to allocate suboptimal amounts of resources to research. Second, state action is also of crucial importance because the innovation process itself is an inherently collective endeavor. As such, innovation is iterative and cooperative in nature; therefore, there is a significant role for public actor sin facilitating, enhancing, and maintaining innovative activities. Third, the state must actively link the local industry with global markets, both production networks and financial markets. Lastly, in each specific industrial sector, the state and industry need to be able to manage constant change. State actions and policies that prove successful in early stages of the industry's development might prove harmful in later stages. Specifically, the development agencies need to be able to manage the political reality of their own diminishing importance as the industry grows.[12]

Breznitz's point cannot be overlooked: the government has a role to play in picking industries. Steve Denning, a columnist at *Forbes*, wrote in August of 2011 an article titled "Why Amazon Can't Make a Kindle in the USA." He made note that the "U.S. has lost or is on the verge of losing its ability to develop and manufacture a slew of high-tech products. Amazon's Kindle 2 couldn't be made in the U.S., even if Amazon wanted to."[13] Why? Because the industries Amazon needs—"flex circuit connectors ... electrophoretic display[s] ... wireless card[s] ... controller board[s] ... Lithium polymer batter[ies]"—have long since migrated to Asia.[14] In many cases the skills and industrial infrastructure to manufacture these products never existed in America. Experts like Denning and Breznitz understand the government has a role to play. Because the government of the United States was not involved in building and implementing a plan for ensuring our high-technology jobs stayed in the country, those jobs went elsewhere, leaving the myth that these would replace blue-collar manufacturing jobs nakedly exposed. Here again the election of Donald Trump looks less and less a surprise. One of his talking points has been why America cannot be the home of these manufacturing jobs. He is not wrong to have asked the question, even though the party whose nomination he won had blocked every attempt to craft a strong national industrial policy.

Steven Rattner, writing in *Foreign Affairs*, addressed why Germany's economy has been able to weather the 2008 global financial storm and maintain a vibrant export-driven economy. As he sees it, "when it comes to boosting exports, of course, the need to maintain or even increase the size of the manufacturing sector, in particular, has been an article of faith in major developed countries for decades. Politicians and voters alike believe that having companies that 'make something' is a key element of economic success, in part because manufacturing jobs have historically paid above average wages. For its part, *Germany embraced manufacturing, and much of its economic success is thanks to that decision*" (emphasis added).[15] Rattner's article highlights the dynamic that needs to exist between government and private industry, a linkage that Germany has had for many years but that the United States largely has not. Cynics of the broad financial-engineering industries that have accumulated so much power in America point out that if American government policy were as tightly linked with manufacturing as it is with Wall Street, the country's industrial sector would be much more robust than it is now, a lesson which seems appropriate given Germany's success.

The fifth and final myth, that economic growth for the world would offset the economic dislocation of the American middle class, is simply the accumulated effect of all the previous myths. In the face of occasional resistance to the idea that free trade was the right course of action for Americans, it was common to hear the refrain that "a rising tide lifts all boats." The idea was that even if we felt some short-term pain resulting from the economic dislocation of industries moving offshore, it would be offset by the new opportunities for growth that would present themselves in emerging economies. The hope was that American companies could export from the United States in China and other BRIC nations, which would in turn create American jobs. In fairness to advocates of this, our current recession would be much more severe if we did not have the opportunity to export to China. In 2016 American companies exported a record $169.3 billion to China.[16] This is great news, but it must be coupled with the fact that in that same year we imported a record $478.9 billion from China.[17] This sort of imbalance speaks to the heart of the myth that by selling into China and helping its economy flourish, we would create enough economic opportunities to replace those lost to lower-wage countries.

Is China partly to blame for America's current economic anxieties? Certainly. But China is primarily to blame only in the sense that the bulk of America's economic policy-making capacity was directed at facilitating globalization in ways that benefited big business without similarly paced and scaled incentives to foster well-paying jobs for American workers in both low- and high-technology sectors who would be negatively impacted by globalization generally and a normalized trade relationship with China specifically. China has become a placeholder for rage Americans need to direct somewhere. While it might be emotionally satisfying to blame China for problems entirely of our making, it will do nothing to resolve the underlying problems and in fact may well destabilize the modern world in ways that will make everything harder, in particular for those already most negatively impacted by globalization.

None of this suggests that China's economic practices during this period have all been consistent with their international obligations. China's economic growth owes much to policies that are blatantly nationalist or what some have called mercantilist. These are policies designed to provide their domestic manufacturers with a wide range of incentives when they export to Western markets. These incentives range from subsidies for Chinese producers to tax rebates on certain goods and to Beijing's policy of a fixed exchange rate between the U.S. dollar and the Chinese Yuan that has made Chinese goods artificially less expensive than they otherwise would be if the exchange rate were allowed to float on the open market. None of these polices are new. In fact, they have been China's modus operandi since the country began its process of opening in the late seventies. This, in part, illuminates why the Chinese feel misled. Jobs we once did not want are now jobs we want back; policies we once allowed China to take advantage of are policies we now take exception to.

As a country that prides itself on long-term strategic thinking, China finds this confusing and frustrating. It would be safe to say that this turnaround on our parts has led many in China's leadership to view American politics as lacking sound judgment and long-term vision. Perhaps most important of all, it raises the question in their minds as to whether they can trust the American model. After all, over the past thirty years China's path forward has largely followed in the footsteps of the American embrace of free market reforms; they have followed our lead! If we now want particular industries back, what does that say about the model China was so invested in emulating? Chandran Nair shared with me that in his discussions with political leaders in China, they express dismay over America's economic collapse. According to Nair, to them "it is as if our masters did not really know what they are doing."

For Americans the challenge in the face of our current problems is to choose between the two competing visions. One, the path that the country has been on since 1972, argues that a rising tide lifts all boats, that what is good for China will ultimately be good for America. Advocates of this argument believe that America's economic future is built on low-labor, high-value technology manufacturing and services. Most important, this point of view argues that the current period of economic dislocation should not upend the progress in U.S.-China relations. The other path is one of nationalism and protectionism. Advocates for more assertive nationalist trade policy, such as those in the Trump administration, believe it would send a strong message to the world that America needs to draw lines around certain industries for its own economic well-being and national security. American politicians and policy makers can be broadly characterized in two basic groups: those on one hand who believe the United States can compete and win against China and those on the other who believe China plays by unfair rules, cannot be trusted, and represents a worldview antithetical to American values.

As the world commemorates the centennial anniversary of World War I, we should not forget that precious few of the Europeans who were most impacted by that war had the ability to see the ominous gathering of storm clouds across the European continent that ultimately led to regional and world war. So too does America's political dysfunction, economic malaise, and deep insecurity today hold the potential to again ask for the ultimate sacrifice of many innocent lives. Such an unnecessary conflict would likely have, at its foundation, misperceptions and distrust intentionally stirred up by manipulative politicians who would rather see China blamed for problems of our own making than deal with painful reforms within our own government.

America's political dysfunction, economic insecurity, and cultural fragmentation hold the potential to create an environment in which conflict with China becomes the rational choice of Americans who view China as the cause of their problems. Clausewitz made famous the idea that war was never irrational; rather, it was a sensible choice given the politics of the day. In the aftermath of a presidential election that saw the rise of a Republican president who repeatedly and belligerently blamed China for America's economic challenges, the idea that America would determine conflict with China sensible is not a stretch. In fact, such a conclusion is consistent with the tone and distemper of the 2016 election.

American society is more angry, fragmented, and polarized than at any time since the Civil War, and these frustrations require a near-peer competitor against which they can be released. Americans harbor deep insecurities about our economic future, our place in the world, our response to terrorism, and our deeply dysfunctional government. Over the next several years, each of these four insecurities will be perverted and projected onto China in an attempt to blame that country for errors entirely of our own making. No country has the economic reach or more clearly represents a competitive political ideology than does China. American insecurity has the potential to lead it to be the destabilizing force in the world as it tears down the modern era of globalization, blaming China for its—and much of the developed world's—problems.

For now, the multinational business community remains one of the last bulwarks preventing this unstable world from becoming reality; however, more multinationals are experiencing problems with reliably accessing the China market. This leads them to support more aggressive posturing against China, language that is easily misunderstood by the American public as support for a more belligerent stance against Beijing. Unfortunately, hostility toward China will be one of the lasting themes the GOP takes from the 2016 election and further embraces going forward. The white nationalist and alt-right part of the Trump campaign have limited traction nationally; however, Trump's success in channeling American anxiety against China and globalization has legs. The GOP's traditional base of supporters, once the bastion of free trade, has already begun to turn on China, especially as the multinational community asks for sharper lines to be drawn on trade and as China veers more toward authoritarianism.

War with China is possible but not inevitable. But conflict with China does become more possible by the day, as the dysfunctional American political system refuses to address long-standing issues that plague our government, economy, and culture and that leave Americans insecure and disenfranchised, both keys to the success of dangerous demagogues. This deep insecurity as to America's place in the world, the answer to the question anxious Americans ask themselves as they watch our political theater—"if we are not a great power, then what are we?"—is the next topic to which we will turn.

6

Insecurity over Our Place in the World

"You're still a superpower, ... but you no longer know how to act like one."
—David Rothkopf, quoting a Middle Eastern diplomat, "National Insecurity,"
Foreign Policy, September 9, 2014

For Americans today, the hubris-filled days after the fall of the Soviet Union are gone. Today, the country faces a newly assertive Russia, a dysfunctional Middle East, and a China that is increasingly willing to go its own way. Few things have made America's place in the world more insecure than how we reacted to 9/11. The events themselves could have been only a terrible national tragedy, a consequence of life in an open society, but the U.S. reaction to 9/11 set in motion a process that has exposed the limits of our power overseas, our domestic political system, and our culture itself. Since the 2008 financial crisis, the world has watched as the United States has become less and less sure of itself, fears that by 2016 led to a presidential election that dismayed the world and sent a clear message that America was close to spiraling out of control.

During the Obama administration, these fears accelerated as President Obama attempted to argue for a nuanced approach to complex foreign policy matters, one he framed as "don't do stupid sh— [stuff]."[1] Obama's pragmatism required him to acknowledge that while America's ideals would retain their special place, the reality of what America could and could not achieve domestically or overseas had to be paramount in the decisions he made and the policies for which he advocated.[2] His approach to both domestic and foreign policy rejected statements that could be slapped onto a bumper sticker. Obama was all about nuance and complexity, precisely at a moment when many Americans were hungry for someone who would cast a muscular vision of the country's economic, political and global future. Where Obama embraced uncertainty, viewing it as an essential part of governing wisely, he governed a country desperate for anything but. Americans remain deeply insecure over how to engage the world, which is why voices as disparate as Donald Trump, Bernie Sanders, and Rand Paul are all able to channel these insecurities through policies that advocate increased isolationism. Yet Americans hate to look weak, especially given our collective memories of victory in the Cold War and deep cultural belief that we were the essential great power whose influence drew both world wars to a close.

These uncertainties and insecurities all take place within a world that is characterized by more competing regional powers—often referred to as a multipolar world—at a time when miscalculations and triangulations between countries grows more complex by the month. That America's political leadership in 2017 has a tenuous grasp on any ideas of sufficient complexity has allowed this to become a prime moment for overreaction on the global stage. The recent trajectory of American politics, as perfectly expressed in Donald Trump's administration, has ensured that our former treaty-bound allies are already reconsidering their own obligations to us and to one another.[3] President Trump's May 2017 trip to speak at NATO, where he consciously refused to reinforce his commitment to the treaty's Article 5 on collective defense, led German chancellor Angela Merkel to publicly acknowledge that the time had come for European countries to protect themselves without the treaty commitments that have bound the continent together peacefully since the end of World War II.[4] Countries such as Germany, Japan, and South Korea now recognize they can no longer be entirely confident that the United States will be forever willing to protect them. Going forward, each must reevaluate and ensure they can address the unique regional threat that is China. Among the reasons these countries can no longer count on the United States is that the United

States remains deeply uncertain of what its remaining power can do: what are the limits of whom we can make follow our lead, of whom we can bend to our will?

How did these deep insecurities over America's place in the world come to be? After all, for decades American culture permeated the aspirations of nearly everyone; around the world we were more than just the materialistic envy of the world, we were a political and economic model that almost perfectly captured and channeled humanity's best impulses toward individual and collective success. But now Americans carry themselves with significantly less confidence. Where this comes from, what it means, and where it leads us and the world remain questions with which the world must reckon.

To understand the source of this deep underlying anxiety that permeates much of American life, it is important to go back to where America was when the policy of triangulation between America, China, and the Soviet Union began. Arguably one of the greatest successes in foreign policy history, namely the end of the Cold War without global conflict, unleashed a peace dividend that American leaders—for a brief time—used wisely. But then came 9/11 and with it the unfortunate perfect storm that aligned a dormant worldview, that of the neoconservative, with a profound sense of public anxiety over why all of America's power could not either prevent 9/11 or bring an end to conflict. In the years after the invasions of Afghanistan and Iraq when the limits of American power were available for all to see, not as evidenced in a military shortcoming but rather in the much more profound idea that democracy was neither inevitable nor always possible, America's understanding of its place in the world grew more uncertain. This has all led to a period of global disorder, as perfectly expressed in the strained alliances across Europe and Asia and the ongoing nearly apocalyptic events unfolding in the Middle East. Even as academics and pundits struggle to determine how the Trump presidency came to be, it should come as no surprise that an American public deeply insecure over the country's place in the world would find a politician who promised to "make America great again," someone they were willing to give the opportunity to do just such a thing.[5]

AMERICA'S VIEW OF CHINA DURING THE COLD WAR

America's insecurity over its place in the world is a shame, if for no other reason than it misses the point that today's multipolar world, in which China is economically successful and working its way toward becoming a responsible global stakeholder, is a direct result of a carefully crafted policy by the American government to achieve these very goals. This can be put much more simply: America won. But success carries with it a burden to stay sharp, to not become complacent now that victory has been attained. It is impossible to understand why America's attitudes today betray so many insecurities as to our place in the world without looking back to the Cold War and the priority American policy put on any strategy that could contain the power of the Soviet Union and prevent the further spread of Communism. While America had bigger and nobler goals around normalizing relations with China, there was an equally important goal of using China as a means of triangulation between the United States and the Soviet Union. American policy was oriented around a simple idea: do business with whomever we needed to in order to isolate the Soviet Union. On paper this made a lot of sense; in practice at times it led to America doing business with nations and leaders we would not have otherwise. But the existential threat of Communism and the Soviet Union also meant American politicians would engage countries in the Pacific, Middle East, Africa, and South America, which the United States would later come to regret.

America's eagerness to prevent Moscow from building a relationship with Beijing meant it could count on Washington going the extra mile to ensure trade policy was bent favorably toward China's interests. In fairness to those in Washington who were the most vocal advocates of China's favored treatment during this period, the reforms China's leadership was putting in place during the early eighties gave good reason to believe that China could be successfully divorced from its Communist past. American policy makers believed they could wedge themselves between the two Communist countries: while the Soviet Union and China might have shared similar ideologies, they also had shared histories marked by acrimony and conflict, the seeds of which gave hope to Americans eager to see China permanently align itself with American interests.

Many now assume that because the Soviet Union and China were both Communist countries, they shared a deep ideological connection. That is a mistake. Mao had a long and stormy relationship with the Soviet Union's Communist leadership. Always the egomaniac, Mao did not like the international attention Soviet leadership was given as the perceived bellwether of the world's Communist movement. As the originators of Marxist-Leninist thinking, the Russians would always bear the intellectual Communist mantle. Mao's poetry and political ramblings, the ubiquitous Little Red Book studied by all Chinese in school, was his attempt to put forward an ideology uniquely his own. He wanted to author ideas that would stand alongside the writings of Marx, Lenin, and Engels. As China's unquestioned leader and unwilling to share the spotlight with anyone, Mao found it difficult to line up as one of Moscow's client states.

This tension was obvious early. Stalin wanted to assert his primacy while Mao wanted to assert that of his China—a new country that would greet the world victorious over the KMT, China's nationalist opposition party. Philip Short, in his biography *Mao: A Life*, writes of the first major policy meeting between the two: "Relations with Russia were the cornerstone of Mao's policies toward the rest of the world. If they continued to be based on Chinese subservience, what had the revolution achieved?"[6] Mao would prove too cagey for Stalin, one of the few relationships Stalin could not bend to his will or break with force, a realization he had almost immediately upon this first encounter with Mao.

Stalin and Mao would ultimately find ways to work together, largely at the frustration of the West, but the underlying distrust and animosity between them would never go away. In a 1958 meeting with Pavel Yudin, the Soviet ambassador to China, Mao made this clear: the Soviets "have never had faith in the Chinese people, and Stalin was among the worst."[7] After Stalin died the new Soviet premier Nikita Khrushchev found dealing with Mao even more problematic. Trying to put his country back together in the aftermath of Stalin's disastrous rule, Khrushchev initially played it cool toward Mao, which only infuriated Mao further. Specifically, Khrushchev reneged on large Soviet-led infrastructure projects that had begun in China during Stalin's rule. He went so far as to withdraw Soviet engineers and technicians from China at the height of these tensions.[8] During this period, in an effort to cool the situation between the Soviet Union and the United States, Khrushchev even disavowed China's first nuclear explosion as an unnecessary escalation of the arms race. Mao was infuriated at this and believed it showed the unwillingness of Soviet leaders to grant China its rightful position of leadership on the world stage. In addition, the Soviet Union loosely allied itself with India during the 1962 Sino-Indian war, a move that greatly angered Mao.

Margaret MacMillan, in her book *Nixon and Mao: The Week that Changed the World* writes, "by the end of the 1960s, Mao and, indeed, what was left of the foreign policy establishment in Beijing were convinced that the chief threat to China, greater even than the United States, was the Soviet Union."[9] Under Khrushchev's orders, Soviet troops had marched on Czechoslovakia in August of 1968 in an attempt to make sure a nascent reform movement in the country led by Alexander Dubček did not spin out of control. This muscular interjection of Soviet power into Czechoslovakia embodied what came to be known as the Brezhnev Doctrine, the idea that the Soviet Union could invade any Communist country in an attempt to prevent that country's destabilization. To Mao, insecure in his ability to withstand a similar move by the Soviet Union, this was deeply unsettling. As MacMillan, channeling Mao's question, asks, "If Soviet forces could intervene in Czechoslovakia, why not in China?"[10]

It would ultimately be Mao, realizing that he could not marginalize or forever have as enemies both the Soviet Union and the United States, who would shift toward the United States as the lesser of the two threats. Mao, great strategist though he may have been, did not foresee that by doing so he would open his country to the sort of reforms that were at loggerheads with his own Communist ideology. As Mao pivoted toward the United States, he found a country eager to receive his friendly posturing. For the

United States, Mao's willingness to engage was the penultimate Cold War victory. Ultimate victory over Communism was still a decade away, but Mao's decision was a major step toward America's ultimate Cold War victory over the Soviet Union. The original policy formulation from the United States toward China was simple: engage China, and China will disengage from the Soviet Union. Coupled with this was a subcurrent of thinking that proved incredibly powerful then and remains equally so now: engage China, and China will liberalize and become more like us. This created the policy framework that brought the United States and China together then and that knits us together even now.

An economic justification (that China was a market U.S. businesses could sell into), together with a political one (China would democratize if the West would engage it politically), was tied to the belief that China presented the United States with an essential strategic buffer against the Soviet Union. Together, these three components—the economic and political justifications and foreign policy—functioned with amazing symmetry and continuity through almost three decades of American presidents. Even in the darkest of hours, as questions about China's ugly authoritarian impulses in the wake of the Tiananmen Square atrocities became unavoidable, American insistence that China would ultimately prove to be a good and trustworthy partner owed its support to these three factors. The problem was that as China evolved, our policy approach to the country did not adequately change. Most important, we did not take the necessary steps domestically to address how China's entry to the world's system of trade and governance would impact America's domestic economy. Through the late nineties to today, our approach to China has been deeply wedded to a framework that was born in the heat of the Cold War.

As is almost always the case, victory brings with it responsibilities. Yes, America was essential to winning World War II, but in the aftermath of that global conflict, American power would have to be deployed around the world in treaty-bound formations to prevent hostilities bubbling to the surface. Similarly, American power proved victorious over Communism, both as expressed in the Soviet Union and in China. With the collapse of these threats, America had a once-in-a-generation opportunity to pivot hard into where it put its time, attention, and money and to ensure that in victory, the spoils were shared fairly across the country, in particular in the part of America that had long borne the brunt of America's foreign policy adventures.

WHERE AMERICA SPENT ITS PEACE DIVIDEND

President George H. W. Bush and British prime minister Margaret Thatcher coined the phrase "peace dividend" to capture what they hoped would happen in the period after the fall of the Soviet Union: rather than spending money on defense, they suggested this money could be spent on research and development, education, social benefits or—always a favorite—reduced taxes. Until 9/11 America did spend gradually less and less on defense directly because of the peace dividend.[11] Lawrence Klein, a Nobel Prize–winning economist, has written that the peace dividend "should be considered the major economic achievement of the 20th century."[12] Expanding on this thought, Klein stated that during the years subsequent to the end of the Cold War, there "was truly a Peace Dividend. The United States achieved full employment, state and local governments went into budget surplus, and the federal government started to retire outstanding debt."[13]

Initially, during the presidencies of George H. W. Bush and Bill Clinton, we used this peace dividend wisely. The prosperity Klein references was also part of why American policy makers felt so confident being aggressive on free trade and timid on domestic industrial policy. Every indicator gave them reason to believe America's economic future was on solid ground. The rise of the Internet economy led politicians to think they could look past structural questions about America's economic transition from heavy industry to high technology. As a result of this misplaced confidence, American policy makers believed they could use free trade as a vehicle for further remaking the world in our image.

The ways in which free markets empower individual liberty were certainly an important insight, and one that has its place, but our leaders gave too little weight to the implications of almost 2 billion Chinese and Indian low-cost laborers entering the work force. No wonder that on one episode of Bill Maher's HBO show, in an interview with AFL-CIO President Richard Trumka, Maher asked whether "the world has enough jobs."[14] This sort of question did not adequately color the pursuit of free trade by American policy makers during the height of the peace dividend. Now that we have spent the peace dividend and gone into serious debt post-9/11, the United States must face the dual threat of high debt and a limited ability to spend money training workers for new industries. It is worth pointing out that an equally if not more disruptive force is now being released as technology accelerates automation to the detriment of workers everywhere. To the extent American domestic economic and political policy paid too little attention to globalization, it is showing itself to be similarly shortsighted when thinking through the societal implications of broad sectors of the economy being automated.

Where did the peace dividend go? According to Klein, "the situation lasted a few years but came to an abrupt halt when the successor government made unusual tax reductions and knocked the economy into recession, abetted significantly by the outbreak of terrorism in 2001. We did, however, enjoy brief experience of a Peace Dividend. Let it be noted that economic life became more enjoyable and manageable during the Peace Dividend period."[15] Simply put: America spent it away, largely in response to the events of 9/11.

The peace dividend was not some limitless resource—in its simplest form it was a fixed amount of money we could choose to spend once until the world's political and economic systems found a new normal and some of America's advantages were competed away. If we had spent it in a way that lowered America's long-term entitlement obligations or improved our economic fortunes, then the peace dividend would have been money well spent. Instead, 9/11 happened. In the wake of that terrible day, the U.S. government sought to accelerate economic growth through a series of major tax cuts and spent upwards of $6 trillion dollars for the war on terror. The wars in Afghanistan and Iraq, the mobilization of the Transportation Security Administration, the expanded role of the Department of Homeland Security and George Bush's 2001 and 2003 tax cuts—these were all choices we made. Their cost made sure that other areas where we needed to make investments—infrastructure, education, health care, technology—did not receive them.

What the United States did with the peace dividend after the end of the Cold War is an important question. It is equally interesting to ask what we did with the political capital—both domestic and international—that constituted a peace dividend in these areas. The end of the Cold War also held the potential to free American policy makers to turn their attention toward other longer-term issues. If ever America had the chance to think long-term and execute meaningful reforms and chase noble goals, it was during the period after the Cold War. How did the United States spend this aspect of the peace dividend?

American politics during the period between 1991 and 2001 (roughly the decade between the collapse of the Soviet Union and 9/11) were marked by five main pursuits: First, the United States spread democracy through free trade to, in turn, empower globalization. Second, the United States made meaningful efforts to reform limited portions of its entitlement programs, focusing initially on alterations to the American welfare system (something spearheaded by Republican House speaker Newt Gingrich and ultimately embraced by Democratic president Bill Clinton). This focus on reforms was coupled with a realistic tax policy that both Republicans and Democrats supported, which led to the first balanced budget since 1969. Third, American politics elevated the role of high technology and service industries as the answer to the question of where displaced workers would find work once globalization began to transfer jobs to lower-cost labor markets. The latter policy, as we have discussed earlier, was given too little thought and was too underresourced to be effective. We are feeling this now as it becomes clear that American blue-collar workers have little to hang their hats on as far as future jobs they are qualified to hold. Fourth, American politics pursued cheap credit with something bordering on fanaticism: partially because it lubricated domestic consumer spending, but also because inexpensive credit facilitated homeownership and because the construction boom that resulted was a surefire way to stimulate the economy. The fifth and last distinguishing characteristic of this period of American politics was a noticeable shrillness that crept into our discourse, something that would make it nearly impossible for American politicians to find compromise in times of crisis. Pettiness incapacitated Washington, leaving it feckless in the face of mounting domestic economic struggles that cry out for meaningful reform, strong leadership, and intelligent policies. While we were growing increasingly fanatical in our politics, China was growing increasingly pragmatic, and the results can be seen: China held onto economic growth as we struggled and became increasingly insecure over our place in the world.

NEOCONSERVATISM MEETS THE AMERICAN PUBLIC

In the short term, America's use of the peace dividend was constructive for U.S.-China relations, even though many conservatives distrustfully watched China grow and accumulate more military power and regional influence. Absent the bogeyman of Soviet Communism, America's foreign policy focused on free trade and international standards of governance, to the great good of globalization. America's peace dividend was largely put to good use until the catastrophe of 9/11. The events on that day would not only give American exceptionalism an ideological counterweight (militant Islam), they would also usher in an era defined by a new idea, that of neoconservatism. But what would the impact of this worldview be on America's foreign policy? How would it impact our relationship with China?

After the collapse of the Soviet Union, many great foreign policy minds such as Jeane Kirkpatrick turned their attention away from how the United States could best defeat international Communism toward how a newly empowered America should use its power. Their answer in the years before 9/11 was to use American power to better the world through humanitarian interventions. Jeremy Moses, a senior lecturer at the University of Canterbury, wrote in a 2007 paper on the topic of humanitarian intervention, "indeed, neo-conservatives such as William Kristol and Robert Kagan were amongst the foremost advocates of humanitarian interventions in the 1990s and were critical only of the perceived failure to use enough American firepower, particularly in the case of Serbia in 1999."[16]

The events of 9/11 amplified and distorted these beliefs in ways that are clear only in hindsight, but much of what drove these thinkers forward originally was the belief that America's peace dividend could be used to better the world and that it had the responsibility to do so. Beyond its argument to use American power on humanitarian grounds, neoconservative thinking in the heat of the months after 9/11 was also firmly attached to the idea that democracy was the ultimate form of government and that America would use force, where necessary, to create free societies. President Bush channeled this idea in multiple public speeches but never more powerfully than when he named the Iraq invasion "Operation Freedom."[17] As the war in Iraq spiraled into a series of disasters and the justification for the war changed, the idea that America had at some essential level a responsibility to bring freedom to the Iraqi people was never far out of reach.

While many historians are quick to point out that America has always had a predilection for getting involved in foreign entanglements, Bush's channeling of neoconservative thinking was different in ways that further confused Americans over their place in the world. For liberals the idea that force could be used to give another country freedom clashed with their idea that societies developed along lines and levels that were not entirely predictable and did not respond to force, even when that force had the best of intentions. For conservatives Bush's policies cut yet another anchoring idea from the core of what it meant to be conservative: if a foreign power (the United States) should go into a country on the other side of the world (Afghanistan, Iraq) to give its people something they have not yet created for themselves, then where are the lines between what people must do for themselves versus what an outside power (i.e., the government) must do on their behalf? The conservative ethos of "pulling yourself up by your bootstraps" was entirely at odds with the conservative foreign policy as expressed by President Bush. Your country does not have democracy? Well then, the United States will give you one. The elevation of neoconservative thinking after 9/11 provided clarity in the short-term because it set up an intellectual framework within which the use of force in Afghanistan and Iraq could be justified, but it ultimately decoupled many conservatives from what had traditionally been an essential part of their belief system: specifically, that you do not do for someone else something they can within their power do themselves.

In the mind of the American public, neoconservative foreign policy crystalized two ideas that have direct bearing on our relationship with China. First was the idea that American power had a role to play freeing people from authoritarian rule. For many Dragon Slayers, the idea that China is ruled by despots fundamentally hostile to American ideals is already taken as truth. Conceptualizing a scenario in which a profoundly anxious American public could be stirred to act on behalf of a repressed Chinese people is not a stretch. Second was the idea that American power should not be constrained to act only after a disaster has occurred but should be able to act preemptively. The doctrine of preemption is prone to extreme manipulation, of which the Iraq War is only a small example. It is worth pointing out that neoconservatives such as Jude Wanniski have long argued for preemptive action toward China, going all the way back to the Cold War era. Wanniski famously said of the possible threat China represented to the United States, "if you look down the road and see a war with, say China, twenty years off, go to war now."[18] Of these two neoconservative contributions to American policy, the doctrine of preemption is particularly dangerous because of the multiple scenarios where Chinese military influence is already challenging American hegemony in places like the South China Sea. Preemption is also particularly dangerous for U.S.-China relations because it is one of the only engagement doctrines with which the U.S. military might be able to decisively defeat China should a conflict in the Straits of Formosa break out. To be more specific, because China has surveyed the U.S. military's capabilities in Taiwan and deliberately designed weapons systems capable of swarming and overwhelming U.S. attacks, the only military doctrine available to the United States in the run-up to a conflict is to preemptively strike. This calculus is dangerous because it creates a scenario in which the possibility of conflict makes a preemptive attack by the United States all but inevitable, purely because the United States knows that if it waits to be attacked first, it might not be able to protect its military assets in Taiwan or the Straits of Formosa.

OUR RESPONSE TO 9/11

In 2017 America is a country deeply uneasy about its future and its place in the world. Since 9/11 our understandable paranoia over what comes next has fueled a constant stream of fear-inducing movies, television, and popular fiction. National news programs know they have a ready-made audience any time they choose to run a program on "what could happen if terrorists ___," where the newscaster fills in the blank with: "attack our food supply," "take down our electric grid," "hack into the Federal Aviation Administration," and so on and so on. And terrorists are all too happy to add more fuel to the fire, even if their attacks thus far have thankfully come up well short of what Hollywood and CNN would have Americans believe lurks behind every corner. Our politics has chased popular culture down this same rabbit hole. Real leadership would have elevated our minds and reminded us of the costs of liberty and freedom inherent in an open society. More importantly, leaders with fortitude would have reminded us of the extraordinary safety Americans enjoy. These fears have built to a crescendo at the same time America's economy has struggled. As our collective unease has grown, our politics have cheapened, leaving America a fragile democracy.

America's sense of frustration and insecurity toward China is not unique. We harbor a similar foreboding about our relationship with the Muslim world. There is a real collective anxiety about how to greet Islam, an unease felt more acutely in the aftermath of the 2011 Arab Spring. These events were greeted with much hope, only to see America's aspirations again crashed on the rocks of societal reality nested deeply within countries that few in America really understand. We have had to realize that many of the new governments do not have constructive attitudes toward Western values of pluralism, the role of religion in government, or the treatment of women. Overall, the seemingly constant unfolding of disaster in the Middle East frustrates Americans not only for that region in particular but for the idea that freedom is something to be valued over order, an idea with immediate application in the Middle East and China. Add to these insecurities our attitude toward China, and it is obvious that America greets with deep unease the major influences that will shape the twenty-first century.

American hegemony was always more than a pure military phenomenon. Since the end of World War II through what many historians believe will be measured as the apex of American hegemony—the end of the Cold

War—the twin features of America's hard and soft power combined to create a unique force for good. While our military power remained the world's best, our cultural power has diminished. Following the 2008 financial crisis, the extent to which American culture relied on an exaggerated and unhealthy version of consumerism has been exposed for all the world to see. The debt most American families carry to afford a lifestyle only the wealthy in emerging economies could imagine has made foreigners suspicious about whether America's affluence has made it soft, unable to rise to meet the challenges of the twenty-first century. And in the heat of our shared anxieties and fears after 9/11, America's culture wars have intensified to points not seen since the Civil War.

TURNING ON ONE ANOTHER

Our dinner tables, where we break bread with friends and family, have become battlegrounds. Political disagreements push apart well-meaning individuals whose worldviews are rarely as incompatible as either Fox News or MSNBC would have us believe. Friendships become strained, and many dissolve entirely with nothing more than political disagreement to blame. We have been marketed outrage for the last twenty years through talk radio, 24/7 cable news, and the post-truth information vacuum that is the Internet.

But while these media reflect our emotional responses to the issues we face as citizens, they do little to help us understand where to locate our current politics against historical precedent. If we accept that each of the previous descriptions captures how a wide swath of the electorate on both sides of the aisle feels specifically about the other and about domestic politics generally, can we create a more meaningful answer that will help us then move toward productive disagreement, discussion, and new solutions? For our politics to move forward constructively, we need to understand four themes that, when combined, provide an answer to the question of why U.S. politics has become so destabilizing to America's understanding of its place in the world.

First, in the United States we have elevated discussions about rights well above any parallel discussion over responsibilities. If America's first original sin is slavery, its second is enshrining so much of our founding documents in language that emphasized our rights in opposition to established power without commensurate mandates as to our individual responsibilities. This flaw strikes both conservative and progressive causes equally. Reframing any discussion about our rights as Americans should require a complimentary answer to what responsibilities attach themselves to the exercise of those rights.

The traditional political narrative on the topic of rights and responsibilities is that conservatives understand this balance better, and to the extent that essential conservative politics emphasizes personal responsibility as an ultimate good, this is wise. Missed by progressives is that conservatives understand there comes a time and place in every individual's life where it is on them to act and to take responsibility for themselves. We can and should recognize that this moment of truth will be different based on education and opportunity, but to never require individual responsibility is to miss a fundamental insight into human nature and what the individual must commit to in order to break destructive cycles.

Progressives dismiss conservatives' fears both of an entitlement state's disincentivizing individual agency, as well as most people's experience interacting with the faceless and nameless bureaucracy that is big government. Conservatives trivialize the idea that solutions to certain messy social problems, like education, homelessness, or health care, may not be particularly efficient, and in thinking they can be, set government up to fail. Having said this, progressives' own views on responsibilities are often trivialized by conservatives. Progressives do not necessarily disagree with the conservative point of view on personal responsibility; rather, they emphasize responsibilities they see between social groups that exhibit asymmetries of privilege. Progressives feel society has a responsibility to seek out ways to provide opportunity for the disadvantaged. On this topic conservatives have superior messaging: the argument that personal responsibility always trumps collective responsibility allows cleaner lines to be drawn around what can and cannot be done to better another person's situation. If you are poor, you are not a hard worker. If you are uneducated, it is because you did not seek an education out. It begins and ends with the individual. Progressives push back and in doing so argue for more grace and collective assistance because they see certain struggles as playing out in a social context that is not an individual's making. Yet in doing this, progressives struggle to define precisely when enough help is enough. In this tension conservatives can draw a clearer line than progressives around where help should begin and end; however, these two points of view are fully compatible. No small wonder that against the backdrop of all these disagreements, many average Americans feel lost and disconnected from their country and one another.

In fact, the best policies toward thorny questions around poverty, education, and health care should reflect mutual insights from both conservatives and progressives. Conservatives should argue for the individual's responsibility while progressives should argue how to construct a setting within which this exercise takes place. Competent politics would acknowledge that the line between individual and collective responsibilities will shift over time, and as such, metrics should be established that allow policies to change as the facts on the ground change. This approach would be wise, and it is within our reach.

Second, both American political parties have moved to the right post-Nixon. Judged by the standard of what constituted an Eisenhower Republican, the three best GOP presidents of the last forty years would be Ronald Reagan, Bill Clinton, and Barack Obama. To understand the Tea Party's anger, look no further than their outrage at how the size and scope of the federal government expanded during the last Bush presidency. As Jon Ward put it in a piece for the *Washington Times*, "George W. Bush rode into Washington almost eight years ago astride the horse of smaller government. He will leave it this winter having overseen the biggest federal budget expansion since Franklin Delano Roosevelt seven decades ago."[19] Going back even further, today's movement conservatives have vocalized their frustrations even with President Reagan, under whose leadership the government ran huge deficits and drove up the national debt.

What was Nixon's answer to America's health care problem, as evidenced in his legislation drawn up for Congress? A federal mandate. The conservative Heritage Foundation's answer to President Clinton's single-payer proposal? Mandates and insurance exchanges. The first large health care reform enabled by a Republican governor? Romney's mandate and establishment of insurance exchanges in Massachusetts. We may quibble at how these various proposals were different at the margins from the Affordable Care Act, but they shared more commonalities, both structurally and conceptually, than differences. There was no push, no whisper, of a single-payer model in President Obama's health care reform. In fact, Obama's health care reform was directly lifted from the conservative playbook, something intellectually grounded conservatives such as David Frum had no problem acknowledging. As Frum wrote for the *Atlantic*, "it seemed to me that Obama's adoption of ideas developed at the Heritage Foundation in the early 1990s—and then enacted into state law in Massachusetts by Governor Mitt Romney—offered the best near-term hope to control the federal health care spending that would otherwise devour the defense budget and force taxes upward. I suggested that universal coverage was a worthy goal, and one that would hugely relieve the anxieties of working-class and middle-class Americans who had suffered so much in the Great Recession."[20] Coming from one of this generation's leading conservative voices, a former speech writer for George W. Bush, Frum's honesty about what Obama had proposed around health care was a moment of honesty Republicans wanted nothing to do with.

For those Republican policy folks who in the nineties were writing columns and drawing up positions that attacked the Clinton single-payer model to now see the proposed solution they once advocated for widely reflected in the modern era ACA should have been a victory. That conservatives do not is not borne of any meaningful intellectual insight into health care reform in the years in between; it is the stillbirth of a movement designed to emasculate President Obama at every turn, regardless of whether or not his positions reflect ones the GOP once occupied. This all speaks not only to the reactionary, rightward shift of Republicans but also to a similar rightward shift by Democrats who, by the time the Obama administration had given up on single-payer, had instead accepted the broad outlines of a conservative think tank's approach to health care reform. In the aftermath of a disastrous 2016 election for Democrats, a number have begun to stand up and assert that this drift right, as evidenced in President Obama's approach to health care reform, needs to stop, and that the progressive idea of single-payer needs to be presented to the American public.[21] The abdication of a single-payer system by President Obama was a victory for how conservatives had long argued health care reform should be approached.

Third, American politics has become a zero-sum game. This is dangerous domestically, as evidenced by the response of the global financial markets to the debt limit brinksmanship of the GOP over the last several years; however, this very zero-sum approach to politics will light the world on fire when it inevitably spills into foreign policy and international relations. Our presidential elections thus far have managed to delicately avoid crossing this line, but as evidenced this year, we have now reached the point where politics and actual policy are colliding.

Imagine, if you will, what our relations with Russia would really look like if U.S. political rhetoric became policy, or if certain American politicians had their way and we "made the sand glow" in the Middle East.[22] We may roll our eyes at this type of hyperbole now, but any measured review of the language used in the run-up to and dissolution of the Vietnam War would find similar language. Can we forever keep separate the jingoism of American politicians from actual policy? If we are to make anything of the Trump candidacy, it is that we are closer than ever to political rhetoric becoming policy. This should be as great a source of fear for us as it is with our allies.

Fourth, American politics is struggling to adapt to the reality of a multipolar world. While the United States is without question the global hegemon, our self-perception is that we are in decline economically and politically. Multipolar worlds tend to be more dangerous because they are characterized by a former great power gradually losing its ability to exert control over others. This inability to project power as the nation once could is largely because emerging powers are growing economically and beginning to stretch their legs. Descending great powers, from Rome to the British Empire to the United States today, tend to be marked by domestic politicians who seek to advance themselves by arguing that the opposition is responsible for the nation's decline rather than employing more structural explanations that take into account the wide gap an emerging power must close with the developed world.

Whatever instability is felt by the great power—in our case the United States today—has much more to do with its own insecurity than with the real threat posed by emerging powers such as China. The precision with which past ascending and descending great power politics is playing out in America today versus past times should be cause for alarm. The United States is not above other historical moments of coercive great power politics that have led nations to war. The type of domestic dysfunction America is currently in the midst of is rarely contained within a great power's home turf. It expresses itself externally, in large part because outside actors are easier to demonize and act against than internal enemies.

HATING PRESIDENT OBAMA

In an act some on the left might have labeled as deeply cynical, Beliefnet, a website for evangelical Christians, asked the question a good number of Americans had themselves wondered over the previous eight years: "Why do so many people hate Obama?"[23] Some pointed to race, an acknowledgment that for as much progress as Americans have made since the Civil War and desegregation, racism is still a defining part of the country's cultural and political life. Still, most Americans know someone who despised President Obama but was not racist. Was the reason his supposed liberalism? If so, then why did the bulk of his policy initiatives not project onto a liberal agenda particularly well? Health care is, of course, the best example of this. Partisan Republicans will never admit it (intellectually honest conservatives will), but Bill Clinton and Barack Obama's economic policies were more closely aligned with the worldview of Dwight Eisenhower and Richard Nixon than that of FDR or Lyndon Johnson. A good measure of Obama's pragmatism can be easily found searching through various pieces written by frustrated liberals during his administration. One such essay, labeled "Stop Calling Obama a Liberal," makes this point clear:

In the face of his policy preferences, no rational argument can be made for calling Obama a liberal, progressive or even leftist. Yes, he is to the left of the GOP, but that is because Obama is a center-right corporatist while the modern GOP is a political Frankenstein's monster—created from the right wing fringes of the libertarian movement, Christian right, neo-confederates, neo-conservative war hawks and anarcho-capitalists; saying that Obama is a leftist in relation to these people is like saying that Siberia is in the south relative to somebody standing at the north pole.[24]

In 2010 James Bennet, a writer for *the Atlantic*, noted in dismay about President Obama, "for the left, each day brings more disillusion: Afghanistan; Guantánamo; rendition; no prosecution of Bush officials; immigration; Don't Ask, Don't Tell; a health-care law that, okay, might be the most ambitious social legislation in 45 years, but didn't create a single-payer system and was heralded by a truckling executive order on abortion."[25] A group of political scientists from America's leading universities have come up with a way of measuring Congress and the presidents' views. Their survey showed that "President Obama is the most ideologically moderate Democratic president in the post-war period."[26] Reflecting on the Obama presidency's lack of a muscular expression of a progressive agenda in the summer of 2011, *Salon* columnist David Sirota noted, "Obama isn't weak. . . . He just isn't a liberal."[27] Had Obama been a socialist as many on the right suggested, he had ample opportunities to either break up or nationalize the financial and automotive sectors when he took office—he had inherited the largest economic crisis since the Great Depression. As many progressives will begrudgingly admit, if anything, Obama's economic policies furthered the trajectory of socializing the losses of private enterprises and allowing the upside potential to accrue to the 1 percent. If he was a socialist, he seems to have been a socialist who aspired to help business. Yet the net of many Americans' point of view on Obama was that he was worthy of their hate. If not entirely based in race and if not in politics, then what explains this hatred toward President Obama?

People hated Obama because he had the temerity to acknowledge that America could no longer do whatever it wanted, wherever and however it chose to. What Obama saw as a necessary if painful truth, that America was now constrained to live within the realities of a multipolar world, deeply offended many Americans who still wanted to believe that American power knew no limits. In the aftermath of botched invasions of Afghanistan and Iraq, when the economic might of an ascendant China seemed soon to equal that of the United States, President Obama's foreign policy reflected two essential truths about American power: it had limits, and Americans no longer wanted to be the world's policemen. As is often the case, the leader who is charted to govern under these principles is hated because of them. Obama forced Americans to admit our deep insecurity that our place in the post–World War II world, in which the United States had the ability to dictate to the world how it would conduct itself, would no longer hold. It should come as no surprise that American politics now has been sucked into the vortex of the Trump administration, where bellicosity and shouts of "America First" attempt to make up for a profound insecurity that America is no longer sure of its place in the world or of the limits of what it can and cannot accomplish through sheer force of will.

President Bush and President Obama will be judged poorly by historians. Bush will be judged for a grotesque overreaction to 9/11, the mismanaged invasions of Afghanistan and Iraq, and an acceleration of the economic policies that made every aspect of inequality in American life worse. Obama will be judged poorly for different reasons: namely, an inability to recognize the great danger his own country posed to the world unless it addressed deep structural problems and pragmatism when a bolder vision of how to reshape government to elevate the interests of the common man was desperately needed. Obama's moderation and temperance, both of which are admirable qualities, made it impossible for him to ever be the hard-charging agent of change that his campaign promised and that the country sorely needed. But even more problematic was that his pragmatic nature, while a refreshing difference from the nature of his predecessor, made it impossible for him to hammer home what would have been a traditional, progressive set of policies centered around the idea that economic inequality and the political marginalization of America's working and middle classes were festering problems that could derail the entire republic. This pragmatism carried with it a profound reset for American foreign policy, as the Obama administration began to unwind America's presence in Afghanistan and Iraq.

Of all the key achievements and decisions that allowed Barack Obama to become a viable candidate for president, perhaps none was more important than his public opposition to the Iraq War. Some of that opposition was because he was not actually in Congress at the time and as such was not subject to Washington's unique ability to pervert the judgment of otherwise sensible individuals. But Obama deserves some credit for recognizing that the arguments being used to support an invasion of Iraq came up well short of justifying it. Obama encountered two inevitable problems the moment he became president: being against the war was not the same thing as having a plan for what to do now that we were in it, and articulating a new "Obama Doctrine" was going to require more than "don't do stupid stuff." Obama did not get the United States into either Afghanistan or Iraq, and where blame is to be assigned it should categorically be directed toward President Bush's administration. However, as these wars unwound, Obama struggled to articulate a compelling worldview that made Americans feel secure. He was tactically precise in his foreign policies but strategically absent a unifying worldview. After all, "don't do stupid sh— [stuff]" is every president's foreign policy. What Obama was missing was a coherent foreign policy that allowed friends and foes to predict the lines that would trigger America's wrath.

Gideon Rose, writing in *Foreign Affairs* in late 2015, noted that

> The president is variously painted as a softheaded idealist, a cold-blooded realist, or a naive incompetent. But he is actually best understood as an ideological liberal with a conservative temperament—somebody who felt that after a period of reckless overexpansion and belligerent unilateralism, the country's long-term foreign policy goals could best be furthered by short-term retrenchment. In this, he was almost certainly correct, and with the necessary backpedaling having been accomplished, Washington can turn its attention to figuring out how to get the liberal order moving forward once again.[28]

This point is essential: what Obama and his supporters may have missed is not that they were intellectually misguided but that they were emotionally disconnected from something essential to the American spirit and in so being set the stage for another muscular reaction to a collective insecurity over America's place in the world. Even after Vietnam, Afghanistan, and Iraq, a core part of American culture is the belief that our country is somehow fundamentally responsible for being the guardian of freedom and democracy. While foreign misadventures may temper public enthusiasm for wars of choice in the short term, the losses thus far have not made isolationism an essential component of American politics. In publicly advocating for the United States to acknowledge what it can and cannot accomplish, President Obama unleashed a deep torrent of hate, not because people thought he was wrong, but because they feared he was right.

Across Middle America, President Obama's seeming admission that the United States would need to admit to the limits of its power was deeply unsettling. If America's politicians were no longer able to come together to build economic policies that benefited the average American, if democracy was this dysfunctional and unproductive, and if America's military could no longer act with impunity to democratize the Middle East or constrain a reassertive Russia and a newly emerging China, was America safe? To make it all worse, in the period following 9/11, the sporadic events of domestic terrorism again and again whispered into the American ear, "you are not safe, you are not secure, and your government cannot protect you."

7

The Amorphous Threat of Terrorism

"Bin Laden's greatest triumph, however, may be economic. In 2004 he claimed his ultimate goal was to bankrupt America. . . . The U.S. federal debt has tripled to over $17 trillion since 2001. The never-ending war on terror has absorbed trillions from the U.S. economy. . . . The nation responsible for leading mankind to the moon now chooses to spend its money on over 3,000 domestic intelligence organizations and not on new dreams of reaching Mars."

—Scott Gilmore, "How the War on Terror Is Killing America," *Maclean's*, September 10, 2014

The terrorists are winning. We can feel it in our bones. Not because of the physical damage they inflict; no, the damage is more intangible, an effort to turn the West in equal parts against itself and Islam. A war against Islam will be as harmful as any conflict based on people's religious affiliation must be; a war between the West and itself will be catastrophic and very much what the terrorists hope to achieve. While I was working on this chapter, a terrorist reportedly affiliated with ISIS detonated an explosive at an Ariana Grande concert in Manchester, England. Security appears to have been just good enough to have kept him from entering the concert area itself but not good enough to prevent him from finding a concentrated group of people where he could detonate his device. The explosion killed over twenty people, several of them children. A couple of weeks later, while I was editing this chapter, my iPad screen displayed a message saying British police were responding to reports of a van attack on the London Bridge. Several months before, a truck plowed through a crowd at the Berlin Christmas market, killing twelve and leaving more than fifty with serious injuries. Few have forgotten the tactical precision with which, before lunch time on January 7, 2015, the offices of *Charlie Hedbo* in Paris were assaulted, a dozen people executed at near point-blank range, and another eleven wounded.

Moments like this have become a more common aspect of life in Western Europe and, to a dramatically lesser degree thus far, with the notable exception of 9/11, the United States. In between each of these assaults were others, equally random in their timing, tool of terror, and targets. An evening holiday celebration, the middle of a busy workday, the morning rush into the office; a bomb, a truck, an assault weapon; an off-duty British soldier walking down a London street, a commuter on the morning train, young people dancing at a club. Our minds abhor randomness, and because acts of terror are designed to be inherently random, terrorism robs us of our ability to think rationally. When danger looms behind every trash bin, every backpack, every truck, it becomes impossible for societies to calculate risk. A country that has lost its ability to weigh the use of force or the role of the police or the need for mechanisms to prevent government from taking away personal liberties is precisely the outcome terror is designed to achieve. The consequence of this inability is not limited to how the West views Islam; rather, the mid-term repercussions of terrorism will become one of the key insecurities that make global conflict in general, and between the West and China specifically, more probable.

The people behind these terror events know something essential about Western media and society: the 24/7 news machine must be fed. The babbling media pundits who need to tear each other down and the perfectly coiffed TV anchors are of little value to their employers absent stories that circle around shared traumas and feed on collective neuroses. Terrorists are all too happy to provide us with such stories: they deliberately feed our shared fears, and they do so knowing we will rip ourselves to shreds debating how to rationally respond, when neither today's news media nor the events themselves make any effort to be anything other than perversely irrational.

With each event, the West's collective ability to dispassionately assess risks and require of politicians commensurately measured responses diminishes. Each terrorist attack brings the West closer to the very sort of overreaction bin Laden himself hoped to provoke the United States into, a response he believed would show how shallow the West's commitment to freedom and pluralism was. In the days immediately after 9/11, David Plotz, a writer at *Slate*, pointed out, "bin Laden has strategic reasons to believe in terrorism, too. The Muslim victory over the Soviet Union in Afghanistan showed him that superpowers are not so superpowerful. And the ignominious American withdrawal from Somalia—following a Bin Laden connected attack—convinced him that the United States is morally weak. The U.S. soldier is 'a paper tiger' who crumples after 'a few blows.'"[1] Fourteen years after 9/11, Tom Engelhardt would caustically write,

> So let's give credit where it's due. Psychologically speaking, the 9/11 attacks represented precision targeting of a kind American leaders would only dream of in the years to follow. I have no idea how, but you [bin Laden] clearly understood us so much better than we understood you or, for that matter, ourselves. You knew just which buttons of ours to push so that we would essentially carry out the rest of your plan for you. While you sat back and waited in Abbottabad, we followed the blueprints for your dreams and desires as if you had planned it and, in the process, made the world a significantly different (and significantly grimmer) place.[2]

Linda Bilmes, an economist at Harvard University, calculated in 2015 that the wars in Afghanistan and Iraq would cost the American taxpayer somewhere between $4 and $6 trillion, or to say that more plainly, more than either World War I or World War II had cost the United States.[3] As she writes, "the large sums borrowed to finance operations in Iraq and Afghanistan will also impose substantial long-term debt servicing costs. As a consequence of these wartime spending choices, the United States will face constraints in funding investments in personnel and diplomacy, research and development and new military initiatives. The legacy of decisions taken during the Iraq and Afghanistan wars will dominate future federal budgets for decades to come."[4] And yet even today as the consequences of America's disproportionate response to 9/11 come more and more fully into focus, the country's ability to demand of itself and its policy makers a certain toughness, a willingness to absorb a certain amount of risk unique to the threat of terrorism in open societies, and instead direct this money, human capital, and policy-making wherewithal toward bettering America's education, health care, and infrastructure remains a pipe dream. Terrorism has stolen the American Dream, it has robbed the country of its ability to elect wise stewards, and perhaps most unfortunately, it has lain the groundwork for an emotional, anxiety-ridden overreaction against a country more similar in form and function to such past nemeses as the Soviet Union rather than the fragmented terrorist organizations who jump from one war-torn country to the next, always trying to stay out of reach of America's spy satellites and cruise missiles, weapons designed for near-peer conflict, not blowing up terrorist campsites.

The modern age has seen its share of terrorists causes come and go. Europe and the UK weathered a series of terror attacks from the seventies to mid-nineties, largely from a variety of left-wing and separatist groups. So too has Israel, with its troubled history of terror attacks by Hamas, Hezbollah, and others. A study of terrorist attacks in Europe by the *Washington Post* found, "From 1970–2015: 4,724 people died from bombings. 2,588 from assassinations. 2,365 from assaults. 548 from hostage situations. 159 from hijackings. 114 from building attacks. Thousands wounded or missing."[5] American life in the 1970s was rife with terror attacks, a point Bryan Burrough made clear in a piercing essay in *Time* magazine:

> It may be hard to recall now, but there was a time when most Americans were decidedly more blasé about bombing attacks. This was during the 1970s, when protest bombings in America were commonplace, especially in hard-hit cities like New York, Chicago and San Francisco. Nearly a dozen radical underground groups, dimly remembered outfits such as

the Weather Underground, the New World Liberation Front and the Symbionese Liberation Army, set off hundreds of bombs during that tumultuous decade—so many, in fact, that many people all but accepted them as a part of daily life. As one woman sniffed to a *New York Post* reporter after an attack by a Puerto Rican independence group in 1977: "Oh, another bombing? Who is it this time?"[6]

It is hard to imagine Americans today being this sanguine about terrorism, no doubt because the scale of what transpired on 9/11 suggests to most people the destructive potential today's terrorists are capable of. However, somewhere American culture and political life need to align on the realization that terror is not new to open societies and that the ideal of perfect safety has never been the reality, even in the United States. This historical lens serves as an important reminder for Americans that modern Western societies have always been vulnerable to the threat of terrorism. What has changed are two things: first, the fear that nuclear weapons technology has proliferated and could be accessible to terrorists, and second, that a virulent strain of militant Islam has taken flight across the world, deliberately seeded by enormous quantities of money in societies with rampant youth unemployment, profound disillusionment with the modern world, and a deep sense of unfairness at the world's dispassionate response to their suffering.

America harbors an especially unique fear over nuclear weapons. Hiroshima and Nagasaki do not hang over American life because there is any consensus these cities should not have been decimated in the world's first use of nuclear weapons during World War II; no, the destruction that ensued has fed a deeper fear that in opening the Pandora's Box of nuclear war, America will at some point be on the receiving end of a type of weapon it first developed and used. The threat of terrorism in American life today is uniquely damaging not because we are purely focused on the lone wolf or even the coordinated attack like what took place at *Charlie Hedbo*; no, what Americans fear right here and right now is that a weapon it unleashed on the world will finally find its way back to our shores, and that in some sad way, this would be the universe's blood debt required of anyone who unleashes such a terrible weapon an another. As misguided as such a thought would be, it does capture an essential insight into why Americans are so uniquely fearful of a nuclear weapon being used domestically.

Absent the unique insecurity over nuclear weapons in the hands of terrorists, America's fears over Islamic terror should not reach the same levels as those in Europe, given the EU's proximity to the Middle East and the number of immigrants the EU currently hosts from Muslim countries. Since the 1980s, many of Europe's immigrants have been from predominantly Muslim countries.[7] This accelerated with the war in Syria and the rise of ISIS, with over half a million refugees fleeing Syria to live in the EU.[8] In October 2016 the Pew Research Institute noted, "European Union countries plus Norway and Switzerland received a record 1.3 million refugees in 2015, accounting for about one-in-ten of the region's asylum applications since 1985. About half of refugees in 2015 trace their origins to just three countries: Syria (378,000), Afghanistan (193,000) and Iraq (127,000). Among destination countries, Germany (442,000 applications), Hungary (174,000) and Sweden (156,000) together received more than half of asylum seeker applications in 2015."[9] On its own, this amount of inbound refugee traffic would be difficult to absorb and would likely result in extremism from those displaced from their homelands who are unable to build new identities and who turn to fundamentalist religion as a result. Unfortunately, this recent wave of refugees happened during a period when long-standing rifts between the host countries and European Muslims who have never fully integrated into the West have begun expressing their fundamentalist beliefs through acts of terror. Europe has a real problem both with so-called home-grown terrorists and with those who came as refugees and who may never integrate into the West. Making the whole problem worse is that across Europe, postmodern thinking of which the left has been particularly guilty has struggled to weed out voices of extremism from within its own borders. History will not look kindly at countries that played host to Muslim radicals, turning a blind eye to their rhetoric of hate for the West as the Muslim world burned and terrorism became more common.

Even though Europe's problems with Islam and terrorism are much more immediate and frequent than those of the United States, Americans remain fixated on terrorism as a threat to themselves and their loved ones. Numerous studies have tried to make the point that no rational calculation of risk would lead to Americans being as fearful about domestic terrorism as they are.[10] The most useful insight around what Americans should actually be afraid of—the pervasive presence of guns in circulation across the United States—seems to be largely ignored. Americans are more likely to die from gun assault (1 in 358) than by foreign-born terrorism (1 in 45,808). John Mueller, author of *Chasing Ghosts: The Policing of Terrorism*, said of the risk calculus that drives how Americans think about terror attacks, "I once asked a guy at [the National Institutes of Health] how much we should spend on preventing a disease that kills 6 per year, and he looked at me like I was crazy."[11] The difference between how western Europe and the United States responds to terrorism is a function of any number of things, but two are most important: the fact that in recent history America's wars have all been outside its own borders and the unique trauma of 9/11. Europe still has a deep cultural memory of two world wars, and England in particular prides itself on, as British friends put it, "a stiff upper lip." America does not.

Because terrorism is random, most people can project themselves and loved ones into hypothetical casualties. This type of projection is further fed by the media, and it becomes a special type of corrosive fear that leads people to support aggressive actions by the government and police. In addition, because terrorism is inherently barbaric—the backpack bomb packed with steel balls, a beheading, a point-blank execution with an assault rifle—it provokes in people a deep desire for revenge, and a very particular type of revenge, one that will use force and even torture in furtherance of retributive justice. While these all feed on our emotions, terrorism does one other thing that is essential: it shows the limits of what government can do to protect its people, and in exhibiting this limitation, people become willing to give up more personal freedom in the interest of feeling safe. But giving up these freedoms will not be enough to keep Americans safe, and as domestic anxieties spread from those of personal safety to personal economic security and a pervasive sense of loss as to America's role in the world, the electorate will be increasingly willing to listen and respond to politicians who offer up some other entity against which these insecurities can be directed. In the next decade, the combination of a public weary from the constant threat of terrorism and the perfect alignment of China as the only country in the world that poses a political, ideological, economic, and military threat to the United States will lead American politicians to argue for a more aggressive posture toward China that could well spell the beginning of another world war.

While each of the previous insecurities this book has discussed has an intangible cultural component, the amorphous threat of terrorism uniquely taps into America's collective and unique cultural insecurity because of 9/11. In the aftermath of 9/11, American society felt a visceral need to strike back. This response had to be as impactful as possible, which was why the Bush administration's plan to use America's military to invade Afghanistan was politically saleable to a traumatized public searching for a way to punch back. But this use of military force proved unable to resolve the trauma of 9/11. Washington still had at its disposal significant political capital and social willpower to do "something" else in response to bin Laden's attack. In *Chasing Ghosts*, Mueller and his coauthor Mark Stewart note of other countries around the world that have experienced terror attacks,

> although political pressures may force actions and expenditures that are unwise, they usually do not precisely dictate the level or direction of expenditure. Thus, although there are public demands to "do something" about terrorism, nothing in those demands specifically requires American officials to mandate removing shoes in airport security lines, to require passports to enter Canada, to spread bollards like dandelions, to gather vast quantities of private data, or to make a huge number of buildings into forbidding fortresses. The United Kingdom, which faces an internal threat from terrorism that may well be greater than that for the United States, nonetheless spends proportionately much less than half as much on homeland security, and the same holds for Canada and Australia. Yet politicians and bureaucrats in those countries do

not seem to suffer threats to their positions or other political problems because of it.[12]

The American psyche, for all its wonderful offerings to the world and its peculiar insights about human nature, is uniquely vulnerable to the threat of terrorism. Because of this, American domestic and foreign policy will always be uniquely overreactive in fear of terrorism. After the invasion of Afghanistan, while I was back in Indiana with a couple of friends, we were discussing the pending invasion of Iraq. As the conversation went back and forth over the merits of invading Iraq, one of my friends leaned back, threw his hands out in front of his chest, and said, "I don't care if Iraq was involved in 9/11, and I don't even care if they have weapons of mass destruction (WMDs). I just want to see us hurt somebody." He was not alone, and the Bush administration knew it.

Justifications for why America invaded Iraq are many; however, few would question that America's shared psychology when the Iraq War was sold to the public was to flex our muscles and retaliate. This point is crucial: terrorism provokes in the average person a belief that their government should be able to protect them, and when it cannot, they turn to that same government and its available force to do more to make them feel safe. What should have kept us out if Iraq was not just Colin Powell's Pottery Barn Rule of "you break it, you buy it."[13] What should have kept us out of Iraq was an awareness that terrorism is always the tool of those with power asymmetrical to that of its victims: a country using fighter jets, cruise missiles, and stealth bombers to respond to an act of terror is signaling to the world that it has lost the ability to rationally respond to the unique threat terrorism presents to an open society.

In the period after the invasion of Afghanistan, America's collective wounds led to desire for a state-on-state response that initially took us to Afghanistan but ultimately led us to Iraq. Intentionally, or as part of the same anxieties Americans all shared, the George W. Bush administration tapped into this vein and produced one of the original arguments that led America into Iraq. In the months following 9/11, a tenuous relationship between state-sponsored terrorism and Saddam Hussein was enough to get Americans to support an invasion. While the linkage here is ostensibly related to terrorism, the deeper connection is that America's military machine needed another near-peer competitor against which to turn its wrath. This same psychology is playing out today, as Americans grow more and more fearful around how to respond to domestic terrorism. The all-encompassing, never subsiding fear of terrorism is fatiguing American society in the same way it has calcified our politicians' ability to develop thoughtful responses. This is terrorism's goal and real purpose: to fatigue a society to such an extent that it becomes irrational and behaves as such. But where will these insecurities go? Another war in the Middle East? No. As bad as America's collective memories are, the country understands all too well how little return on investment the United States can get there. Russia? A convenient enemy, and one whose conduct during the 2016 election should make it a prime candidate for America's hostility. But for Russia to be seen as America's enemy would require of many partisan Republicans an acknowledgment that Russia acted on their behalf. And given that Russia's economy is in shambles and that it is a demographically dying country, the likelihood it will remain a great specter capable of channeling America's frustrations and need for near-peer competition remains small. Rather, America's cumulative nebulous insecurities will be packaged up and redirected toward another country that represents an economy, political system, and near-peer military power that is competitive with America. The only country that fits all of these criteria is China.

In ways that require the sort of imagination too few of our political leaders have, the events of 9/11 shed light on how an equally anxious America could respond to China. For every deep subject matter expert who knows China intimately well, the idea that the United States and China are bound for war is perceived to be naïve. And yet how many of these same people misread how Americans' profound anxieties would lead them to support Donald Trump? The trauma of 9/11 led America's politicians and policy makers to turn up the heat on potential threats to American security. A similar escalation with China as the target is hardly outlandish. Within conservative camps in particular, a sense remains front of mind that the United States' foreign policy has become naïve and has

looked past clear and present dangers. Renewed efforts have been made
to identify additional sources of terrorism from nation-states, and the idea
of preemptive war has already been elevated as an option that America
should make use of. As President Bush said in the run-up to the war in
Iraq, "facing clear evidence of peril, we cannot wait for the final proof—
the smoking gun—that could come in the form of a mushroom cloud."[14]
The linkage here is critical: a terrible act of terrorism on 9/11 led not only
to a war in Afghanistan, the country that had hosted bin Laden, but
directly to a fundamental change in America's war doctrine, one in favor
of preemptive war with another nation-state. Terrorists armed with box
cutters had successfully taken down not only two of America's landmark
skyscrapers, they had also successfully pivoted the whole of America's
military doctrine in ways that future unscrupulous politicians will be
able to use to steer the country toward conventional near-peer nation-
state war. There are few ideas more insidious or amenable to dishonest
use than the doctrine of preemptive war. World War I saw this idea used
to justify Germany's attack of France and Russia on the basis of the latter
two countries' "inevitable" threat to Germany's sovereignty and ability
to defend itself. World War II saw the idea of preemptive war used by
Japan to invade Manchuria and by Germany to defend itself against Polish
terrorism. The doctrine of preemption is at its most dangerous when it
is hosted by a country and people deeply insecure on a variety of fronts.
The aftermath of 9/11 took America to Afghanistan and Iraq. A version of
America even more unsettled and deeply anxious going to war with China
in an effort to again feel good about its place in the world is not hard to
see, and it would exist well within the same ideology and temperament
that led America into the Middle East.

But an even more important question must be asked: what happens
to America if terrorism never becomes the sort of existential threat it has
been held up as? What if all of Hollywood's terrorism-fueled blockbusters
prove to be cultural masturbation, a sort of fiddling while Rome burned,
a distraction from much deeper and more insidious threats to America's
legitimacy that were entirely of our own making? When an existential threat
like terrorism that has absorbed massive amounts of money, manpower,

and policy-making bandwidth disappears, where does all this bureaucratically fueled fear go? The reflexive answer is that this would make another U.S.-led round of conflict in the Middle East unlikely (which is not to say conflict in the Middle East is unlikely—it is anything but); yet America's memory of the inability to get anything done and of making everything worse in Iraq is a hard boundary within which future action in the Middle East is likely to be contained.

What must be asked is whether terrorism has fatigued America's ability to perceive a more basic existential threat within its own borders, a coalescing comfort provided by authoritarian political figures who promise clear enemies against which American power can be asserted. America may well find itself at odds with Chinese power, but whether or not such a moment escalates into global war may have more to do with American political dysfunction than real aggression on the part of China.

8

America's Dysfunctional Political System

"It turns out there is a consequence for political dysfunction. That consequence
is Donald Trump. Which is to say that, of all the many forces behind the rise
of Mr. Trump and Trumpism, one of the most important but least discussed
is partisan gridlock in Washington. A lot of Trump support is rooted in the
simple and utterly nonideological idea that he will get something done,
even if it's hard to be entirely sure what that something would be."

—Gerald F. Sib, "How Political Dysfunction Fueled the Rise of Republican
Presidential Candidate Donald Trump," *Wall Street Journal*, May 9, 2016

In 2016 when Donald Trump secured the Republican nomination in my
home state of Indiana, I was devastated. In 1993 I ran for and won my first
position as a College Republican in Indiana. Two years later I would run
for and win the College Republicans state chairmanship. During that
time I advised for, worked in, and supported a number of Republican
campaigns as a disciplined conservative. I met my wife on election night
in 1994 at an event for Senator Richard Lugar; she was a leader in the
College Republicans at Butler University, and I a leader at the state level.
I participated in the conservative leadership program at Morton Black-
well's Leadership Institute, a well-thought-of training ground considered a
requirement for any future conservative leaders. I held roles at the national
level including at least one ill-fated Republican presidential campaign.
I authored my share of conservative articles, arguing for approaches to

environmental regulation, foreign policy, and health care that in hindsight seem more compatible with the views of Barack Obama than of George Bush and completely outside the gonzo world of Donald Trump. But in the midst of the Gingrich Republican revolution it became obvious something was amiss.

Temperamentally, the Republican Party in the mid-nineties began to drift more and more toward a particular type of zero-sum game politics, as evidenced in the Gingrich-led government shutdown of 1995. Strategically, the shutdown was designed to force reforms around government entitlement spending and thereby address a long-held conservative fear specific to the nation's debt. Tactically, the shutdown was an expression of how Republicans would approach the negotiation of contentious political issues in American life: nothing was purely a matter of partisan differences; everything was an existential matter of life or death, the continuation or closure of the American republic. And even more problematically, the idea that the use of any means possible, even if the means approaches violated long-held bipartisan norms, was acceptable if it furthered conservative ends. Today it is possible to draw a direct line from this first Republican-led government shutdown to the dysfunctional Congress of the last twenty years, one that in May of 2017 had a 20 percent approval rating from the American public and that has forced both Republican and Democratic presidents resort to executive actions to get anything of substance done.

Doctrinally, in the aftermath of the Cold War, Republicans and Democrats were equally unmoored. Communism focused the conservative mind as few other existential threats had the potential to do. Conservatives understood the great ill that was Communism and brought forward unique insights around human nature, how we act as individuals and as a collective, and why free markets matter in response. Democrats pivoted hard into social and cultural issues at the same time they began to push away from the concerns of working Americans, as evidenced in particular by President Clinton's embrace of globalization and the inadequate safeguards his administration put in place for workers hurt by the economic dislocations that followed. After the collapse of the Soviet Union, the lowest-hanging fruit that offered a set of alternative orienting ideas were social issues. Republicans and social conservatives ran headlong into the culture wars, accelerated by an American evangelical church that had since the sixties been uncomfortable with the postmodern nature of American ethics, values, and cultural relativism. During this same period, Democrats and social progressives saw the opportunity to address what they viewed as long-standing prejudices unique to the American experience around race, gender, and sexual orientation. Postmodernism crept into the progressive worldview in ways that prevented Democrats from clearly identifying which traditions were a danger to an enlightened and pluralistic society and which ones posed real existential challenges to Western society. The danger here on both sides was that in making social issues primary, Americans were pitted against one another as more than just fellow citizens with different political views but instead as opponents whose differences were certain to lead to the end of Western civilization. Republicans argued that same-sex marriage would mean the collapse of Western civilization at the same time Democrats asserted conservatives were rejecting core principles around pluralism. This was a process that by its very nature was going to foster animosity and encourage demagoguery. Here too Americans today can make a clear connection between the culture wars and a toxic political environment in which too many equate someone's spiritual identity with their party of record.

Ideologically, Republicans grew comfortable "doing" politics by taking defensible positions to extremes. At its core this was an embrace of fundamentalism. Free market fundamentalism would enable global markets for capital and labor while giving too little thought to the domestic economic dislocation, and therefore the likely populism, that would ensue. Why? Because free market fundamentalism holds that things sort themselves out. The second amendment morphed from a uniquely American right and responsibility to become a fundamentalist fetish, as expressed in pornographic displays of assault weapons, silencers, and high capacity magazines. A coherent and honorable conservative belief, that the limits to what government can do well must be recognized and honored, became a fundamentalism that government can do nothing well. As emerging economies across Asia and within China in particular experimented with industrial policy and aggressive state-led investment in science, technology, and infrastructure, U.S. Republicans loudly fought against similar efforts while free market fundamentalism accrued more and more benefits to capital and fewer and fewer to domestic workers made insecure by globalization. Foreign policy fundamentalism proudly severed itself from a legacy of conservative realism and instead embraced a highly interventionist, preemptive doctrine of engagement that was completely at odds with any disciplined conservative worldview. In the vitriol and heated anger of the Trump campaign and now his administration, America now has a line of sight on where fundamentalism always leaves its followers: a world well short of the promises it has made, and as such, a world not worth defending but rather of tearing down. Trump's candidacy is the beginning of this, not the end.

Democrats did themselves no services during this period. The party began to distance itself from the concerns of its traditional constituents. This process began, oddly enough, when the so-called New Democrats began to poach particular ideas about globalization, organized labor, and entitlement reform from traditional conservative thinking. The Clinton administration happily took the view that moving to the middle and taking up positions once anathema to traditional Democratic constituents such as welfare reform, globalization, and tax policy was the path to victory, and they were right. But the New Democrats did not anticipate that their move to the right would drive Republicans even further to the right, nor did President Clinton's movement recognize that they had badly missed the mark on what it would take for the average American to benefit in the mid- to long term, given the pressures of globalization and automation. Reflecting on a passage from *Primary Colors*, a novel that is widely understood to be a study of Bill Clinton's campaign, in which the Clinton-esque figure levels with a disgruntled worker about the need to "go back to school," author Thomas Frank captures how the New Democrats turned away from their working-class constituents in the early nineties: "What workers need . . . is to be informed that, in the face of global markets, there's nothing that anyone can do to protect them. That resistance is futile. That only individual self-improvement is capable of lifting you up—not collective action, not politics, not changing how the economy is structured. Americans can only succeed by winning the market's favor, and we can only do that by proving ourselves worthy in school."[1] For a party that once channeled the deepest anxieties of America's blue-collar workers to come to this point was a betrayal of something essential to America's politics. In addition, Democrats began to see identity politics as the end-all, be-all of their political fortunes, overlooking the painful truth that identity politics ultimately fragments society and can unwittingly lead to a cheapened sense of what it means to have a shared citizenship with others. In addition, as these fragmented identities recoalesce into accepted lifestyles in the United States, those formerly disgruntled voters who have traditionally seen Democrats as their only political advocates will begin to have the same concerns that have long motivated traditional Republican voters.

With all this in mind, the 2016 presidential election makes much more sense. It even becomes possible to see Donald Trump and Bernie Sanders as opposite sides of the same coin. Trump channeled economic and cultural populism through the Republican Party; Sanders did the same with only the tools of economic populism at his disposal. Having channeled both economic and cultural populist rhetoric in order to win the 2016 election, it should surprise no one if in twenty years, the Republican Party looks more like the Southern Democratic Party of the early 1960s than anything Goldwater would recognize. Neither Trump nor Sanders are particularly competent stewards of the times, but they both reflect something essential about the American body politick: it no longer believes those in Washington understand their concerns or work on their behalf. The Trump administration is a proxy for something much worse yet to come: a willingness of the American people to turn their backs on every tradition, every norm, and every political principle in the pursuit of someone who will tell them how to make their anxieties and insecurities go away, and who can be blamed when these policies fail.

Our political worldviews are inherently flawed because we are inherently flawed. Religions of all types recognize this and articulate it most commonly as some form of original sin, but freethinkers also see the same problem, communicated as the limits of human knowledge. They overlap in more ways than either camp would care to profess, demonstrating that our worldviews are fundamentally incomplete. This recognition should create humility, but as expressed in our politics today, it instead presents as insecurity. We cannot disagree with those on the other side of the aisle; we must vilify. We cannot negotiate with the opposing party; we must hold to winner-take-all positions regardless of the cost. We cannot learn from others an ocean away because to do so would be to acknowledge the limits of our particular worldview. We cannot accept reasonable limits to positions that define us because we cannot grasp that those on the other side might not be the rigid ideologues that we are. This vilification of one another will burn itself out, and when it does it will need another receptacle into which its anger can be directed.

The conservative worldview offers meaningful insights into the nature of individual responsibility, the danger of debt, and cultural relativism, to name just a few. The liberal worldview offers contrasting insights around why the limits of what individuals can do for themselves requires policies designed to offer a helping hand, the need to recognize that being different doesn't mean being morally, ethically, or spiritually wrong, and that for things to stay the same, they have to change. The debate between these two points of view should be robust—even heated—but the foundation of such interactions must be a mutual recognition that neither side has it all right. Even more critically, our discourse needs to recognize that it is in the actual doing of politics that the best of both worldviews is brought forward and incorporated into actual policy.

America's political system faces questions of increasing complexity at a time of decreasing capacity to discuss, process, or develop policies in response. Every aspect of American political discourse is marked by rabid hyperpartisanship. One of the few areas where people on both sides of the aisle appear to be able to find consensus is that China has hurt the American worker and that it represents a threat to American power. While these impulses have always been a small factor in Washington's politics, the toxic environment has led to few people who want to and are capable of governing to pursue elected office. As politicians in the United States become more rabidly partisan and less interested in governing or helping to make hard policy choices, the American system becomes more prone to overreaction. Few areas are more ripe for this than in U.S.-China relations, where multiple long-standing rationales for conflict will begin to sound more sensible to the ears of those uninterested in hard choices, who are looking to further distract Americans.

Common culture has begun to reflect America's insecurities about our domestic political fecklessness and the perceived ability of China to do nothing wrong. The cult-classic movie *Red Dawn*, originally made in 1984, showed how a group of plucky teenagers led by Patrick Swayze escaped a Soviet invasion of their rural American town. The group, named after their college football team, the Wolverines, hides in the Colorado Rockies, where they fight an insurgent campaign against the Soviet invaders. It may seem quaint now, but at the time America was deeply insecure over its ability to fight off the Communist threat. The Soviet Union had recently invaded Afghanistan, which many in the West believed signaled a newly belligerent and expansionist Kremlin. The Reagan administration had dialed up the rhetorical heat with the Soviet Union, which was reflected in common anxieties many Americans had over whether conflict was inevitable. We can now look back and realize that the Soviet Union was actually in its death throes, but that was neither obvious nor a common interpretation then. Swayze's on-screen band of warriors reflected both our insecurity and the national spirit we hoped we would be capable of summoning if the need arose. That a retread of this movie, headlining Tom Cruise's son Connor, would be made in 2012 is no coincidence. This time, as was originally envisioned by its Hollywood producers, the rugged group of teenagers found itself battling the Chinese, fighting them off in urban Detroit. What symbolism: China had replaced the Soviets, and the inner city of Detroit had replaced the majestic Rocky Mountains.

In a plot twist few could have envisioned, a major change to the updated *Red Dawn* was announced in mid-2011: North Korea would be replacing the Chinese as the invaders. Why? Because international distributors of the film were worried China would blackball their other films from distribution in China if the Chinese were portrayed as invaders. Additionally, Hollywood directors who needed access to Chinese investors for their increasingly expensive films could not afford to alienate the Chinese. This change did not require reading the tea leaves; China's anger over being cast as an invading force was loud and public. The Chinese, having heard about the movie and aware of the deep insecurities it would feed in the United States, expressed public dismay. A columnist for the Chinese newspaper the *Global Times* wrote, "Concerns over foreign invasion have never ceased in the U.S. It is intriguing that China has replaced the Soviet Union to become the top potential enemy causing fear in the U.S."[2]

Beyond examples from America's entertainment culture are those from the media. In 2008, a series of TV ads sponsored by the advocacy group Wake Up Wal-Mart provided an excellent example of the distrust many Americans feel toward China. Run during the busiest holiday shopping season, from Thanksgiving to Christmas, the ads were sponsored by the United Food and Commercial Workers Union. Set against ominous imagery and music, one ad began with the following statement: "America's largest corporation stocks its shelves with products made in Chinese factories while more and more American factories are forced to shut down. Behind those prices Wal-Mart likes to brag about: countless American jobs lost overseas. In this race to the bottom, Wal-Mart gets ahead, and the middle class gets left behind. America can't afford it any longer."[3] The attack was ostensibly about Wal-Mart, but the majority of the language and imagery emphasized China and its threat to America.

Language that blames China for America's problems comes regularly from news outlets like Fox News and CNN. Such pundits as Lou Dobbs regularly attack China, arguing that we have no business engaging the country given its trade policies, human rights record, and Communist ideology. In Dobbs's world, "Communist" tires and "Communist" toothpaste and "Communist" toys have no business being in American homes.[4] In some ways these attacks are not new, but they increased in frequency after the 2008 financial crisis and the 2016 election. Kid Rock tapped into this vein in his 2017 music video "American Bad Ass" when he literally shot a Chinese-made BBQ out of the air.[5] Americans who in the nineties may have been secure enough in their own economic fortunes to listen but not be persuaded are now sufficiently anxious. Many are economically insecure and others are jobless. They not only question whether China can be trusted but also want their leaders to do something about their concerns. The American political system remains extremely prone to overreaction because the people who are responsible for its politics and policies are acutely aware of how unsuccessful they have been providing solutions to the country's most pressing challenges.

The Congressional Budget Office estimates that "federal debt is now equivalent to about 74 percent of GDP, a higher percentage than at any point in U.S. history except a seven-year period around World War II."[6] Early in 2011 outspoken analyst Meredith Whitney publicly announced that she was anticipating a wave of municipal bond failures in America's not-too-distant future. Her reasoning: the combination of declining state revenues meant the states would be unable to service debt taken on over the past two decades.[7] Whitney also believes that because most states do not have to account for their off–balance sheet liabilities, they are not accurately capturing the drain of future pension plan payments. If her analysis is correct, she has identified off–balance sheet pension liabilities amounting to three times the on–balance sheet debt states have acknowledged.

What can we say about the American consumer? Not in good shape! By April 2017 consumer debt had again reached the same levels as before the 2008 financial crisis.[8] According to the Federal Reserve, since the early eighties America's savings rate has plummeted. By the early 2000s, it turned negative.[9] This had only happened on one previous occasion in America's history: the Great Depression. America's negative savings rate happened again most recently in 2006, during a seemingly healthy national economy. In the face of double-digit increases for housing prices and similar returns in the stock market, who needed to save when your investments were growing at such rates? Most were complicit: business wanted consumers to purchase products on credit, consumers wanted what businesses were making, and banks wanted to profit from both.

In what now seems ominous foresight, the *New York Times* ran a series on consumer debt several months before the 2008 crisis unfolded. They noted, "behind the big increase in consumer debt is a major shift in the way lenders approach their business. In earlier years, actually being repaid by borrowers was crucial to lenders. Now, because so much consumer debt is packaged into securities and sold to investors, repayment of the loans takes on less importance to those lenders than the fees and charges generated when loans are made."[10] We now know this all was a dangerous illusion. The aftermath has meant consumers must begin the long process of adjusting their spending habits, paying down debt, and learning to live with the fact that certain purchases are simply no longer in reach.

The combination of consumers and government simultaneously deleveraging will remain a limiting function within the American economy for the foreseeable future. In the aftermath, only the most innovative companies will be able to compete for the increasingly limited dollars American consumers have to spend. Similarly, only the most critical of political priorities will be funded, and even those at diminished levels. The latter will require states to restructure debt, leaving many bondholders in the cold. Debt deleveraging will also make much-needed investments in our deteriorating infrastructure even more difficult to finance.

In the midst of this sort of serious debt deleveraging, sustaining housing prices will be impossible. Since the late seventies, when the idea of buying a house as an investment was first planted, housing prices in the United States have rapidly increased. A house that in 1981 cost approximately $80,000 had increased by 2006 to over $300,000. Not a bad return! But this took the American Dream of homeownership and turned it into a fetish, where the ultimate good became buying as much of a house as you could afford instead of as much of a house as you needed. Since many Americans chose to buy the biggest they could afford, believing it was their best and most important asset, the losses in real estate values across the United States have been extremely damaging to consumer confidence.

The larger reality that the American housing market must come to grips with is not only the loss of perceived value but also three additional factors. First, the American baby boomers are approaching the period of their lives where they will want smaller homes for functional and economic reasons. Second, the cost of capital in the United States and for mortgages in particular will go up and will likely stay up for some time.

While interest rates are at all-time lows in 2017, this will not last. The final policy lever America has in its economic arsenal is to keep borrowing costs low. Like any other policy tool, if used too long this will create problems all its own. In the United States low interest rates further disincentivize people to save, which only adds to the country's debt problem. Rewarding savers requires interest rates be higher than they currently are. Among the primary reasons for a future likely increase in interest rates will be that the United States, regardless of whether we look at government or consumers, is going to have to offer the market higher interest payments to take into account the increased risk of lending in the United States. Third, the American view that every family needs to own a home has changed, with a noticeable inclination toward renting. While some of this may be a short-term response to the housing crisis and collapse in housing prices, the reality is that many Americans see houses they cannot sell as a hindrance to their ability to relocate to parts of the country where jobs are more plentiful. Taken all together, these three factors are going to continue suppressing housing demand for an extended period.

Unhappy American consumers will have another frustration: the all-but-inevitable future of higher taxes. While we should all hold out hope that the American political system finds the fortitude to reform both its entitlement programs and its tax policies, the events of the 2017 debt ceiling debate suggest that meaningful reform in either area remains unlikely. The political system's inability to find a solution is unfortunate because failure to act sets in motion a last-minute rush in the face of an impending crisis where taxes must be raised as a means of augmenting government's declining revenue. Today both parties can afford to polit-icize this debate because international demand for U.S. Treasury funds remains high, and interest rates remain low. At some point, interest rates will change, and even stalwart conservatives will be forced to deal with the need for increased taxes.

Bruce Bartlett, a conservative economist who served as a Treasury Depart-ment appointee under President Ronald Reagan, has written, "at some point, taxes have to be back on the table as the price that must be paid for profligate spending. Only then will the American people realize that they can't have their cake and eat it too, as Republicans have preached for the last decade. Only when the American people go back to believing that spending must be paid for will they stop demanding something for nothing and put the country back on the path to fiscal sanity."[11] Given Democrats have historically been more comfortable than Republicans with tax increases and given the intransigence over tax increases by the current group of incumbent Republicans, it is likely that only an economic crisis that drives up interest rates and threatens to sever the United States' easy access to the world's credit markets will get Republicans to entertain tax increases. American companies looking at the wallets of their potential domestic customers know the likely increase in taxes facing most consumers means they will have even less of their income available to spend.

In addition, one of the most significant headwinds the American economy will face in the next twenty years will be the impact of the baby boomers as they begin to withdraw money from their 401ks, pension plans, and other investments. Expect this to be an orderly transition? While we can all hope for this, the events of the 2008 financial crisis have shown otherwise. Investors who should have been moving out of equities into safer investments were not doing so. The extraordinary and historically atypical returns of the previous years had lulled older Americans into a sense of complacency over the need to rebalance their portfolios as they neared retirement.

The massive conversion of the baby boomers' life savings into health care expenditures will be another headwind for the American economy. Escalating health care costs, tied to the nearly inevitable decrease in government reimbursement, mean the obligation of the individual American consumer to pay for his own health care is going to speak for more of the baby boomers' retirement savings than they originally planned. Cumulatively, the massive conversion of long-term savings into cash will decrease the amount of money available in the American financial system for companies to spend on research and development.

In some ways all of this doom and gloom is the flip side of the unquestioned confidence and unbridled optimism of the last twenty years: that Americans could rely on always increasing house prices and equity markets to fund our consumption and retirement. The fall from grace of these two ideas may speak more directly to America's economic and political future than any other factor. A recent statement on America's economic future by the Economic Cycle Research Institute makes this point abundantly clear:

> More than three years ago, before the Lehman debacle, we were already warning of a longstanding pattern of slowing growth: at least since the 1970s, the pace of U.S. growth—especially in GDP and jobs—has been stair-stepping down in successive economic expansions. We expected this pattern to persist in the new economic expansion after the recession ended, and it certainly did. We also pointed out—months before the recession ended—that because the "Great Moderation" of business cycles (from about 1985 to 2007) was now history, the resulting combination of higher cyclical volatility and lower trend growth would virtually dictate an era of more frequent recessions.[12]

The Economic Cycle Research Institute sees the American economy as being "locked into a vicious cycle." As they put it, "it's important to understand that recession doesn't mean a bad economy—we've had that for years now. It means an economy that keeps worsening. . . . It means that the jobless rate, already above 9 percent, will go much higher, and the federal budget deficit, already above a trillion dollars, will soar."

As of the end of 2015, China held approximately $1.25 trillion in U.S. debt.[13] One of the many newspapers that wrote about this was the British *Guardian*. The daily provided its readers with an interactive chart showing the disproportionate amount of debt China held relative to other countries. As their visual representation showed, China's U.S. Treasury holdings illustrate an important relationship.[14] The fact that China is the number one foreign holder of treasuries is an interesting commentary on China's growing importance. Beijing's investments also suggest the U.S. government will have to be more sensitive to China's concerns than was once necessary, but two much better questions have only recently begun to be asked. First, why does the United States need to borrow so much money, and second, what makes us so sensitive to the amount of treasury debt China owns? This bothers us so acutely because we do not like what owing this money to China represents. Our indebtedness to China represents not only China's rise but also our profligacy and decline; not China's imminent dominance over us but our shortsighted governance; not China's ability to cut off funding but our need to use debt to pay for entitlement programs we can no longer afford. This repressed anger is most easily vented toward China when it really should be directed at the choices we have made that required the debt to be issued in the first place. Much easier to blame China in each of these cases than our own decisions, or lack thereof.

Whether we should be this much in debt—to ourselves, to China, or to anyone—is a much better question. Are we willing to critically evaluate the choices we made as a government and individuals? After all, we are the ones that created the demand for treasuries by spending more than we were taking in. Had China not bought them, we would have needed to pay more interest to attract investors, thereby limiting our ability to spend what we wanted to. The net of China not participating would likely have meant cuts, precisely the sort we see being debated in Washington in 2017. So be alarmed over the amount of debt that China holds, but be alarmed for the right reason: namely, that we lacked then, and still do now, the personal and political will to make better choices that would make us less reliant on foreigners to purchase our debt as a means to maintain our standard of living.

It is worth asking for what America spent this money. From 1990 to 2010, government spending on public pensions (Social Security) and education was fairly stable. Health spending (Medicare, Medicaid) roughly doubled. Welfare spending was down slightly. Defense spending was up (since 9/11, Pentagon spending is up more than double to, as Jim Fallows put it, "levels not seen since World War II").[15] Given the events of 2011 to 2012, none is surprising. How and where we spent this money is important, but equally important is where we did not spend the money: public infrastructure.

The American Society of Civil Engineers has published a report card on America's infrastructure. Their overall grade: D+. Some of the standouts include our drinking water infrastructure (D), levees (D . . . no surprise if you live in New Orleans), roads (D), and wastewater (D+). The ASCE "estimated that in the next five years the nation will invest around $1 trillion in infrastructure—both new projects and improvements, as well as repairs to existing infrastructure."[16] Yet the ASCE estimates that more than double that amount—$2.2 trillion—actually needs to be invested over five years to upgrade these systems. We—not the Chinese—chose to spend the money we raised by issuing public debt in the form of treasuries on tax cuts, entitlement programs, and defense spending, not public infrastructure, as the ASCE report begs of us. Each of these are public goods, and all are necessary, but they are value choices we made for which we are just now coming to grips.

A similar question needs to be asked of the American consumer. Much of the cheap credit phenomenon Americans enjoyed from the mid- to late 2000s was a result of two factors: the emphasis on keeping interest rates low by the Federal Reserve, and the amount of liquidity China's current account surplus has contributed to the world's banking system. Fallows wrote in 2008, "Any economist will say that Americans have been living better than they should—which is by definition the case when a nation's total consumption is greater than its total production, as America's now is."[17]

Fareed Zakaria wrote in the *Post-American World*, "China's lending was also essentially a massive stimulus program for the United States. During the go-go years of the mid-aughts, it kept interest rates low and encouraged homeowners to refinance, hedge fund managers to ramp up leverage, and investment banks to goose their balance sheets."[18] Again, the question has to be asked: if we are now frustrated with the amount of debt we have as households, should we blame China—whose success and thriftiness made this debt available and affordable—or should we look within and blame poor decisions about what we used credit for? Debt is, after all, a tool. To take it on is not bad, but to take on too much for frivolous matters is foolish.

Writing toward the end of his 2008 piece in the *Atlantic*, Fallows had this to say about whether the tenuous relationship between China as a source of cheap credit and American overconsumption could last: "Today's American system values upheaval; it's been a while since we've seen too much of it. But Americans who lived through the Depression knew the pain real disruption could bring. Today's Chinese, looking back on their country's last century, know, too. With a lack of tragic imagination, Americans have drifted into an arrangement that is comfortable while it lasts, and could last for a while more. But not much longer."[19] Anything that cannot last will not. We used a once-in-a-generation moment when credit was incredibly cheap to compensate for stagnating middle-class incomes. We bought bigger and bigger homes, increasingly luxurious cars, and pursued all sorts of nondiscretionary spending previous generations of Americans would have seen as within only the limited grasp of the wealthy. We did not invest back into our communities—unless of course we count the prolific municipal investments in sports arenas—nor did we invest in retraining for the new era of globalization in which new skills and languages will be necessary. These were all choices we made that cheap credit enabled. When the era of cheap credit comes to an end, whom will Americans blame? If the United States chooses to blame China, America will take the focus away from its own responsibility to make wise choices and instead set the world on a path to war.

9

When War Is a Rational Choice

"Men do not fight in modern wars because they like it. They fight because they are told that it is their duty to do so. The clever people invent the excuses for war. The masses are, at worst, taken in by them."

—*New York Review of Books* on A. J. P. Taylor's *Rational Wars*, November 4, 1971

As we did earlier, let your imagination loose for just a few moments. It is 2025, and after two consecutive victories in the presidential election, Donald Trump finally left office in January. America looked very different by the end of that year than it had in January 2016. Trump had proven to be extremely effective at not only dominating the news cycle but also distancing more and more moderate Americans from the political process. As these voices in the middle disengaged from domestic politics, both parties pushed even further into their respective corners. Elections at every level in American politics—from the local to the national—no longer swung on the basis of what the average voter thought. No, those voices had exited the American political process en masse when the Republicans renominated Donald Trump for president in 2020 and when Democrats nominated a West Coast governor that no one in the middle of the country had ever heard of and whose actual experience governing seemed to have a lot more to do with luck, specifically being in state government during a once-in-a-generation economic boom, than skill.

That Trump was reelected by a solid plurality surprised many. What was most shocking was how quickly the passions President Trump stirred up from the left in the year after his election in 2016 dissipated. This was in large part because Trump could clearly tell Americans who to blame for their problems (China) and what they should tear down in order to go back to a time when America reigned supreme. Trump also channeled something essential about American culture, that suffering—whether it be in poverty or health—was in some way the individual's fault. In doing this, Trump's version of Republican orthodoxy elevated the idea that suffering was necessary to purification and that only when people had suffered enough would they be healthy, wealthy, and wise. Trump perfectly expressed a part of America's deep culture for the world to see, something that went beyond the cowboy individualism Americans prided themselves on to an uglier reality that everyone has to take care of themselves because no one else is going to take care of them.

As Trump's two presidencies proceeded, progressives were unable to answer the question of what their vision of government should be. Trump was successful in large part because progressives continued to struggle to put forward a coherent version of what America could look like beyond equality based on race and sexual orientation. Progressives were uncomfortable arguing for more taxes, especially as the 2018 recession drew sharply into focus how tenuous most middle-class Americans' economic situation was. Trump had a commanding advantage: he could clearly tell Americans who to blame and what to tear down during a moment in time when progressives were no longer confident about their own vision for America. As a consequence of this, progressive ideology continued to crash against the rocks, and conservatives continued to rack up win after win until they held such dominance at every level of government, and in all three branches of government, that they could proceed relatively unimpeded toward their ideological ends.

But all was not well for conservatives. Sequential tax cuts had not proven to stimulate the economy as their economic orthodoxy said it would. In fact, economic activity had begun to dramatically decline as immigration was curtailed in 2017, precisely when American economic growth was beginning to be most negatively impacted by the baby boomers' exit from the work force. Only one hundred days into Trump's first presidential administration, it was obvious the multipolar world he had inherited had begun to destabilize, with conflicts in the Middle East and the Ukraine threatening to escalate and draw neighboring countries into war. Overall, the events of the last eight years had led many American businesses to dramatically scale back as foreign markets went into recession and overall became more hostile to the anti–free trade rhetoric coming from Trump's White House. By the summer of 2024, unemployment in the United States was back above 10 percent. Youth unemployment had skyrocketed, and most economists believed the labor participation rate for white American males aged 20 to 45 had dropped to levels not seen since the second year of the Great Depression. A hollowing out of the American Midwest in particular had accelerated, leaving large swaths of rural America empty, with a sense of profound loss of what once was permeating common culture.

Against the backdrop of all this stood China. While China's economic growth had experienced a significant setback in the spring of 2018, largely due to long-standing problems with the nation's debt, under Xi Jinping's leadership China had marshaled its resources, focused, and staggered through. Yes, GDP growth had slowed dramatically from the heady days of the 1990s. But China's megacities continued to swell, infrastructure continued to be built, health care and social services were dramatically better than they were twenty years ago, and China's middle class continued to grow—admittedly at rates slower than the decades before but growing nonetheless. This all led to a renewed sense of pride for China. As American power receded from the global stage, China's power was growing. China now had five nuclear-powered aircraft carriers and delighted in traversing the Gulf of Mexico in the same way American naval power had historically done in the South China Sea. China was first to launch a hypersonic manned bomber, which sent a clear message to the Pentagon that Beijing now enjoyed retaliatory strike capabilities unimaginable a decade earlier. And in an act that proved to be more symbolically powerful than anyone could have imagined, China established a small lunar base in the winter of 2024. Coming at the heels of a domestic economic crisis in the United States that had closed banks and shuttered many businesses that same winter, China's accumulating power seemed to perfectly capture what America once was and what many Americans again wished the country to be.

Throughout his administration, President Trump was always comfortable blaming China for America's economic problems. As America's economic and political problems mounted, this became more common and more extreme. China had gone from being a thorn in America's side that made existing anxieties worse to the direct cause of America's problems. As DC had become more polarized and dominated by the Republican Party, it had become more and more difficult to blame Democrats for America's problems. With each passing day, fewer Democratic politicians had any real say in Washington, which made it nearly impossible to argue that liberal policies were at the root of America's struggling economy. And China had arguably made things worse for America. After all, from 2018 on, Beijing had begun to divest its holdings of U.S. treasuries. This could not have come at a worse time. Interest rates in the United States began to rise precisely as baby boomers looked to cash out the equity in their homes to pay for retirement. As interest rates went up, America's housing market imploded, and U.S. government debt levels sored to nearly 140 percent of America's GDP.

America's suspicions about China's intentions were confirmed not purely by Beijing's relative economic success but more importantly by the Beijing leadership's increasing assertiveness in the South China Sea and toward its neighbors (Russia, Japan, and the newly reunited Korea). Beijing knew that each of these three countries had wronged it in the past, and as such a newly confident Chinese middle class was comfortable pushing around countries that had formerly been hostile to it. War had been avoided, but China and the surrounding area had changed. Japan had turned its back on Article 9 of its constitution and built up its military. Korea was reunited but struggling to merge north and south into one coherent economic entity, let alone one that could defend itself from outside threats. Across Southeast Asia, countries like the Philippines and Indonesia had turned away from the West and instead embraced China.

If America felt anxious about China's accumulating power, Russia was absolutely apoplectic about it. Russia had been in an economic, demographic, political, and military decline since 2018, when Putin had again used force to cement his stranglehold on the country. But Putin's hope for the mighty Russian bear to again present itself was not to be, and he knew his own power and legitimacy was threatened by the successful example of China. Relations between Russia and China had become particularly tense over the last six years as the world watched the two former champions of Communist politics and principles square off against one another. Everyone hoped that calmer heads would prevail, but in December 2025 a deeply marginalized and vulnerable Russia lashed out against China and launched an ill-fated salvo into a disputed border region between the two countries. Rather than acting as an intermediary for peace, the United States responded by supporting Russia, a country that the Trump administration had long held a certain fondness toward. As the United States steamed four aircraft carriers into the heart of the Pacific Ocean toward China, it also nearly tripled the size of its deployment in Taiwan. Beijing had already warned Washington how it would view any additional troop concentration. By April of 2025, when hostilities between America and China finally broke out, it came as a surprise to no one.

Yes, the above is—at least for now—pure fiction. But suggest to many China watchers that any of the above conjecture could be more than just fiction, and they will roll their eyes, confident that the United States and China have more reason to be friends than become enemies. Here again the question needs to be asked: how many of these same voices are only now attuned to what the 2016 presidential election should tell them about their own country? In the summer of 2017, Graham Allison published his book *Destined for War: Can America and China Escape Thucydides' Trap?* Allison, the director of the Harvard Kennedy School's Belfer Center for Science and International Affairs argues that the United States and China are perilously close to reenacting a script he believes characterizes ascending and descending great powers across history, going all the way back to the Peloponnesian War. Many China hands have been quick to attack the book as misapplying the lessons from Greek history to today or not fully understanding what could well limit China's ability to wage the war Allison is worried could transpire. In his review of Allison's book in the *New Yorker*, Ian Buruma points out, "the British historian Michael Howard's remark about nineteenth-century France, quoted in Allison's book, could easily apply to the United States today. The 'most dangerous of all moods,' Howard said, is 'that of a great power which sees itself declining to the second rank.'"[1] Precisely.

Americans would do well to remember now, before it is too late, that it is not preordained we will always do the right thing, or that we will always be the ones who heroically ride in to save the day. We are as capable of the same shortsighted and destructive overreactions to perceived threats, especially in times of extreme anxiety, as countries before us who similarly lost their way. What was special about American life, what made this country and its ideas the envy of the world, is not perpetually renewed. It too can be depleted and misdirected at the hands of political leaders who would rather distract Americans from problems entirely within our control to fix. Think that war with China is impossible? Did you also think that an American president in the modern era would claim China has "raped" the American worker? Exactly how many norms must be violated by the Trump administration for more Americans to recognize that the country is drifting toward a moment where logic has no purchase on America's political consciousness? Where the only way to explain our malaise is to blame another country? Have we, like many who come before, assumed that war is so obviously destructive that it cannot happen again?

In 1899 a Polish economist named Ivan Stanislavovich Bloch wondered aloud whether the machine gun had so fundamentally changed the speed within which a large number of people could be killed in war that in recognition of the horror this weapon could unleash, the continent might never come to blows again.[2] His hope was dashed on the rocks of World War I, when 38 million soldiers and civilians died at the hands of a weaponized military machine Bloch could hardly have imagined. As was touched on earlier in this book, in the decades that followed this great war, another thinker by the name of Norman Angell put forward a version of this hopeful idea in 1933, arguing in his book *The Grand Illusion* that European continental powers should now understand, having seen firsthand the devastation of the last war, that conflict was no means of enriching another country. Angell took great pains to outline how the economic justifications for starting a war made no sense. Angell was proven equal parts right and wrong: right that war would never lead to long-term economic gain but deeply wrong that this would prevent European nation-states from going to war. Like many before him, Angell too had grossly underestimated the human condition: he watched some 60 million people perish in World War II, and the very justification he had convinced himself would forever keep enemies at bay was used by Hitler to justify his annexation of the Sudetenland (Czechoslovakia).

In the aftermath of every war, mankind steps back and wonders aloud how we can prevent such atrocities from ever happening again. We survey the national cemeteries, look at the wounded and the families left behind, and demand of ourselves that we never let such a moment happen again. And yet it does. Again and again men throw themselves at one another, equally committed to their cause and country, equally sure of the justice and righteousness of their actions. And every time as the heat of battle fades, we wonder aloud how humanity could have been guilty of such a moment of irrationality. Yet here is the deeper truth: war is always rational. It is always the sensible choice as understood by the people who stand up and offer themselves at the altar of each generation's god of war. It is rational because their leaders understand two essential things about human nature: insecure people need someone to blame, and blaming an outside actor is always the preferred choice, as opposed to dealing with deeper and more problematic structural problems at home.

Many times war is the preferred option because it is believed to be inevitable. This line of thinking was an essential part of the rationalization used by Germany in World War I, when it projected the economic and demographic gains of Russia and France and convinced itself that only action now would prevent Germany from being overrun. Once the point of view that conflict is inevitable is embraced, the question is not whether war will break out, but when and under what circumstances. In many cases war appears to be rational because it serves to deflect a growing chorus of voices disquieted at the lack of progress or at an acute sense of economic loss, concerns that are more easily laid at the feet of another actor than directed toward internal problems. Regardless of the reason, in each of these moments, war makes sense. Could this be said of a potential conflict with China, that a war with this emerging power makes sense in the near future for the United States because in the not-too-distant future China could emerge as a threat to America's power? Is there a moment coming when it will be sensible to blame China for our own problems and to then set in motion a course of events that will seek to take from China what we believe is rightfully ours? Americans believe themselves to be the saviors of, not the cause of, this type of global conflict, and yet could the same thing not have been said of the Germans in both world wars? In his short book *On Tyranny*, Yale historian Timothy Snyder writes of this misguided American sense of superiority:

> Both fascism and communism were responses to globalization: to the real and perceived inequalities it created, and the apparent helplessness of the democracies in addressing them.... We might be tempted to think that our democratic heritage automatically protects us from such threats. This is a misguided reflex. In fact, the precedent set by the Founders demands that we examine history to understand the deep sources of tyranny, and to consider the proper responses to it. Americans today are no wiser than the Europeans who saw democracy yield to fascism, Nazism, or communism in the twentieth century."[3]

The question Snyder forces Americans to ask is whether our political systems are really that much more robust than those European countries who succumbed to their own blame games and war, or whether our particular era equally prone to express its unique insecurities through conflict.

Political economists Matthew Jackson and Massimo Morelli have wrestled with the question of why rational nation-states go to war. Their survey of world history suggests two reasons why this happens:

The costs of war cannot be overwhelmingly high. By that we mean that there must be some plausible situations in the eyes of the decision makers such that the anticipated gains from a war in terms of resources, power, glory, territory, and so forth exceed the expected costs of conflict, including expected damages to property and life. Thus, for war to occur with rational actors, at least one of the sides involved has to expect that the gains from the conflict will outweigh the costs incurred.... Second ... there has to be a failure in bargaining, so that for some reason, there is an inability to reach a mutually advantageous and enforceable agreement.[4]

What could lead the United States to believe as they put it with respect to China, "the costs of war cannot be overwhelmingly high?" A partial answer can be found in the widely held belief that in recent history America's military has such a commanding advantage over anyone, China included, that we can act with relative impunity. America's misadventures in Vietnam, Afghanistan, and Iraq are largely understood by the public not as a failure of our military technology but of the roles we asked our military to play in countries where guerilla war and not near-peer conflict was the order of the day. Let our military machine lock horns with another country that also has fighter jets, bombers, and armored tank divisions, the belief goes, and all of the problems experienced in Iraq and Afghanistan will go away. The speed with which America's military machine destroyed the Iraqi military in both the Persian Gulf and subsequent Iraq War have lulled too many Americans into the belief that we can escape relatively unscathed from conflict. A conflict with China, even one that occurred purely within the Formosa Straits in Taiwan, would likely dispel this notion quickly. China's military planners have deliberately designed a new generation of weapons that will painfully remind the United States of what it means to engage with a new near-peer competitor who, out of financial and strategic necessity, has consciously thought about how to declaw America's military machine.

But a deeper answer to the question of why Americans might come to believe that a war with China would not result in "overwhelmingly high" costs is that a large percentage of Americans could be easily convinced that stopping China's ascent would accrue economic gains to the United States. This thinking is at the root of many past terrible conflicts, most recently World War I. In his punishingly insightful book on this topic, *Europe's Last Summer*, David Fromkin writes, "Germany deliberately started a European war to keep from being overtaken by Russia."[5] At that time, Germany had any number of reasons to fear a rising Russia, ones that ranged from demographic to economic, but they all played on a central insecurity that Germany could not afford to have a rising power to its east that might threaten its regional power. While we may think today that similar miscalculations are impossible because the stakes are too high, it is already possible to see the fissures that have the potential to push the United States and China into conflict with one another.

Historians have a name for the moment the United States and China are lurching toward: the Thucydides Trap. Coined from a conflict between the two ancient Greek city states of Athens and Sparta, in which the former rose up to assert itself as a newly emerging regional power against the established order of Sparta, this lens has proven a reliable way to predict conflict. In his book on this topic, Graham Allison reflects on cases where a rising power had to engage a declining power. His analysis showed that "in 12 of 16 cases over the past 500 years, the result was war. When the parties avoided war, it required huge, painful adjustments in attitudes and actions on the part not just of the challenger but also the challenged."[6] It is easy to miss the point of his analysis: not that conflict is inevitable but that it is only avoidable when the challenger (in today's world, the United States) is willing to make difficult changes that reflect the new reality. What might we say about how the United States views China? Is this even the best question? Perhaps Allison's point requires a different and more probative question: is the United States capable of such adjustments?

Survey, if you will, the political choices the American public made in 2016 and 2017. Are these choices indicative of a rational, well-grounded electorate, capable of making painful choices around economic and political choices? Or is this an American electorate deeply insecure over its place in the world, its economic future, and the viability of core parts of its governing philosophy? Taking Allison's analysis seriously requires us to admit that conflict with China may be inevitable, not because of any inherent unresolvable tension between the two countries, but rather because the United States harbors profound insecurities over its ability to live with new constraints that govern what America can do without restriction.

Structurally, one of the biggest adjustments that will be required of the United States is to recognize what it means to live in a multipolar world. Coming out of World War II, an essential aspect of America's understanding of itself was that it was one of two global superpowers, the other being the Soviet Union, and that, in the aftermath of the Soviet Union's collapse, the United States stood as the only global hegemon, a country with an unquestioned right to do as it saw fit. But as this book has made clear, a series of dubious policy choices, a couple of ineptly planned and executed wars, and a dysfunctional political system incapable of making hard choices left the United States more comfortable blaming others for its problems than dealing with them ourselves.

America's fiscal problems also pose risks to our soft power, especially given how difficult it can be to substantiate the results of soft power projects. Michael Mandelbaum's 2010 book, *The Frugal Superpower: America's Global Leadership in a Cash-Strapped Era*, points out the limitations the United States now faces when it comes to projecting either form of power. Where once America could "operate free of the need to distinguish carefully between necessities and luxuries," Mandelbaum believes "that era is now ending. In the future, the United States will behave more like a normal country."[7] America's need to dial back on both soft and hard power projects around the world means many of the unwritten expectations about what America would be willing to do, where our country would be able to make its presence felt, and what it can afford to support are going to have to change. The retraction of American power around the globe will create a power vacuum not seen in the world since the end of great power politics in Europe.

Mandelbaum is one of many American thinkers who are concerned about how China will greet America. Will it be a potential partner, or will it act in ways that are at cross-purposes with how the West has structured the world for the last hundred years? Looking back at China's history of humiliation and the resulting animosity the country feels toward much of the existing rule set, which it did not have a hand in making, Mandelbaum writes that China could become "what students of international relations call a 'revisionist power,' seeking to undermine the world's political and economic status quo and replace it with institutions and practices more favorable to itself."[8] The potential for China to undercut the established order does exist and will become more probable as Western powers—the United States specifically—view China's growth as a threat to their own status; however, the reality any nation must face is that its power is not forever ascending. Countries, like people, have periods of plenty and of want. The challenge for countries who find themselves lacking material progress and economic gain is to begin by looking at their own policies for ways they can change before turning their attention outward and blaming others. For countries that choose to look at outsiders as the cause of their problems, protectionism and conflict become likely.

Politics follows economics: when large groups of people become jobless, they demand increasingly extreme political positions from their leaders. When leaders are found to be feckless and bereft of ideas, both leaders and the led will look for someone to blame. In a time of crisis, most politicians possess an appetite for remedies that, in times of greater prosperity and security, would be easily recognized as imprudent. The limitations of America's political class should give pause to anyone who believes that war with China is a ridiculous possibility. Bear in mind that many of these same politicians and pundits were shocked that someone such as Donald Trump could be elected president. We have too many politicians who, being aware of America's problems and feeling particularly impotent to stop them, may look toward a confrontation with China now, when America has a technological lead, in order to halt China's global dominance. It would be convenient that such a push would also distract Americans from the inadequacies of their own government.

The reality of today's multipolar world, in which the United States will have to acknowledge its limits—both for financial and political reasons—is one of less stability. Multipolar worlds have a tendency to be less stable because there is no hegemon to enforce order, and in such an environment, long-standing regional grievances can quickly boil over and, through a variety of unforeseen problems, accelerate from a local to regional to global conflict. To the extent World War II was a continuation of World War I, where unresolved problems between Germany and its neighbors were used as motives for conflict, so too is the Asia-Pacific all too ready for a similar conflagration. Were the United States to determine that conflict with China was inevitable, it would find a number of allies in the region, such as Japan, which has reason to be fearful of China's wrath given how Japan conducted itself in China during the second world war.

In his groundbreaking survey of *Why Nations Go To War*, John Stoessinger reflects on where American attitudes about war stand in the aftermath of two wars of choice: "I believe that the United States presently stands at a fateful crossroads in its history. Empires in the past survived only so long as they understood that diplomacy backed by force was to be preferred to force alone. Once they succumbed to force alone, decline would swiftly follow. The Greeks taught the Romans to call this failure hubris. Perhaps it is not possible for a nation to be *both* a republic and an empire. I believe that democracy is best transmitted to other nations by example, not by war."[9] Stoessinger's caution echoes that of the often-derided Thucydides Trap, that America must not only be wary of hubris but also that war of choice and a great power in decline often go hand-in-hand. America need not be the latter, but as we have already passed through a period of the former, the question of whether American political life is capable of summoning the courage and grace to redirect our shared anxieties away from outside actors and toward choices we must make as a country will be answered with profound consequence in the coming decade.

10

Two Paths Forward

"On the one hand we have Hillary Clinton, a scandal-ridden, uninspiring candidate whose Left-wing policies would destroy what is left of U.S. exceptionalism; on the other is Donald Trump, a demagogue who specializes in whipping up hate and threatening cataclysmic trade wars. This depressing choice comes at the worst possible time for the U.S.: the country is bitterly divided, faith in the American Dream and U.S. constitution is receding and many would like nothing better than to shut themselves off from the world. Meanwhile, the threat of terrorism remains as high as ever."
—Allister Heath, "Donald Trump versus Hillary Clinton," *Telegraph*, May 4, 2016

America has two choices: we can pursue conflict, or we can pursue collaboration with China. A collaborative framework of engagement toward China would not have to be conciliatory or require that the United States turn a blind eye toward China's many failings; rather, it would seek out common ground on economic and foreign policy matters. Collaboration would force America to identify where both countries have shared interests, then make an even deeper commitment to bilaterally binding trade, environment, and military agreements. But for this to happen, America will need to avoid blaming China for structural problems that have taken decades to take root. China is not the reason Middle America is struggling; the inability of American society to recognize and proactively address how global changes would impact this part of the country are. A chronic lack of vision by our political leaders, an unwillingness to sacrifice rigid political orthodoxy at the altar of pragmatic policies and to take political risks deliberately designed to attempt new ways to help average Americans pivot to this new world, and exceptionally poor decisions on where to spend limited human and financial capital are all why Middle America is struggling.

We are seeing something new in Trump. Politics as usual has failed too many Americans, and in their frustration they are willing to act in unpredictable ways, channeling their rage into ideas and actors that even a decade ago would have been laughed off of CNN. Trump has exposed long-standing economic grievances in Middle America that have been trivialized by mainstream politicians from both parties. He has taken advantage of politics as entertainment, a whole form of discourse that markets resentment and outrage. He is certainly not the only American politician to pander to our baser instincts, but he is by far the most manipulative thus far. Absent a unifying ideology other than self-aggrandizement, Trump's daily violation of the norms that have held the American experiment together has paved the way for even more manipulative players who have both much darker agendas and a unified worldview, which will include placing blame on outside actors like China for America's problems. The path of conflict with China benefits from the various ongoing economic difficulties felt by the American middle class, whether those are actually the result of globalization or automation, in particular if their elected leaders prove to be feckless at how to address these concerns. The alternative, a path of collaboration, begins by focusing on those structural problems within American life that are within our power to change: these almost entirely revolve around requiring of our political leaders a positive vision of the future and the ability to make the hard choices we will have to make in order to get there. Today this sort of clear vision is nested entirely within rigid political orthodoxies, ones that do not reflect the lived realities and shared values of most Americans. The central question that may determine whether or not the United States and China go to war will not be China's policies in the South China Sea or its treatment of political dissidents or its trade policies; no, what will determine if the United States and China

lock horns in war will be whether or not Americans again discover political courage and demand of their leaders candor, clarity, and competency.

Everyone understands the stakes if the United States and China were
to become enemies. But too few believe this is possible, another example
of where global elites may be guilty of a tragic inability to conceive of
a world where their ideas are not trusted by the average person. In the
aftermath of Brexit, the 2016 American presidential election, and the deep
insecurities these moments captured, might we today be guilty of the
same complacency as what characterized Europe in its slow march to war
in the years before World War I? Are we really so different and so much
more enlightened that we can avoid the same pitfalls that have occurred
in earlier eras? The globalized world many of us have grown up in, the
one our businesses have invested in and that our economies have become
dependent upon, could collapse more quickly than it came together. Think
this is hyperbole? Remember the ground the world has covered since
2008: the bulletproof American housing industry collapsed, the American
financial system went through a structural crisis not seen since the Great
Depression, and the United States' political system descended into levels
of acrimony and dysfunction rarely before seen, culminating in a 2016
election that sent Donald Trump to the White House. Today, the Eurozone
stands on the precipice of collapse, riven by many of the same economic,
ideological, and terrorism-laden insecurities that America also struggles
with. Each of these should have been a reminder that history is most
certainly not dead, that it is still with us. The lessons of history offer up
warnings about what happens when complacency and ineptitude infect
politics, if only we will listen. The most human of follies and hubris is to
think we are so different from those who came before us, so much more
sophisticated and enlightened, that we can rise above the mistakes they
made and forever avoid global contagion and conflict.

The aftermath of the 2008 financial crisis has shown that America's
economic systems remain vulnerable to mistakes, oversights, and deliberate
manipulation. The aftermath of the 2016 political crisis has shown that
the American electorate is now willing to entertain extravagant charac-
ters, language, and ideas to disrupt a status quo they no longer believe

works on their behalf. The consequences of these realizations should focus everyone's minds on the most responsible path forward before America's political system spirals out of control, taking the global economy and world order with it. America's politicians are resorting to partisan bickering and blaming others for problems created by Washington's dysfunction. Into this volatile mix sits our relationship with China, a country many have long been suspicious of and even more are coming to believe is the cause of our angst. We should not assume it is inevitable that our relationship with China will continue as it has over the last thirty years. We are on the brink of a profound repositioning on how we view China.

As Gideon Rachman pointed out in *Foreign Policy* in 2012, "American-Chinese relations have long contained elements of rivalry and co-operation. But, increasingly, the rival elements are coming to the fore."[1] In 2017—with an American president who wrote in his campaign book *Great Again: How To Fix Our Crippled America*, "there are people who wish I wouldn't refer to China as our enemy. But that's exactly what they are"—the moment in which politicians begin to view China as an acceptable actor to blame for America's problems has come, and with it has come the real possibility of a foundational realignment in U.S.-China relations, one that could well lead to conflict.[2] Keep in mind, the America reflected in Donald Trump's vitriol is not one looking for nuance or complexity; no, this is an America that will want revenge on the country they believe has taken away the security that many across America believed was their birthright. The moment for revenge is not here yet, but it is coming on the heels of the Trump administration's inability to deliver what they have promised. Trump himself is the penultimate existential danger to U.S.-China relations. The real threat comes later, in a candidate who channels American anxieties beyond rhetoric into action.

While America's insecurities mount, our political stance toward China has the potential to grow increasingly harsh. The trifecta that should most worry everyone is when three things align: organized labor (no friend of China's trade practices), U.S. Congress (with its growing bipartisan willingness to view China as hostile to America's interests), and Western multinational companies (whose ability to do business in China is becoming more challenging by the day). When business, labor, and America's Congress sour on China, Beijing will be on the cusp of a more belligerent and hostile America, one willing to disengage with China if the United States feels trade is no longer good for American business. The potential for disengagement also increases if more people on both sides of the aisle in DC begin to suspect that China's prospects for further political reforms are over, or if the American electorate believes ongoing engagement with China is the cause of their trouble.

In the wake of America's malaise, there are two choices: we can turn inward and look toward our policies, institutions, and culture as the most likely places where we can affect positive change, or we can turn outward and focus on the actions and decisions made by other countries toward us that we believe have contributed to our problems. We are much more likely to generate positive outcomes by focusing first and foremost on getting our house in order. Addressing our own problems first is also the most risky and therefore—particularly given our political climate—the least likely to occur. Consequently, it should surprise no one if our politicians begin to focus more and more on outside actors, fixating particularly on China, as the source of much that ails America. Focusing on China is all but inevitable given America's currently limited political vocabulary and the lack of another clear global competitor against which define itself; within such a handicapped point of view, America has two possible approaches toward China.

First, America specifically and the West more broadly can refine our model of engagement toward China and require the country to make additional political and economic concessions to maintain the status quo. Not everything about such an approach would be bad. In fact, there are good reasons to believe that China can today be held to higher standards that it could have been when it was poorer and more vulnerable to political and economic collapse. Second, the United States could treat China's ascent as a threat to our own power. The more our approach to China trends toward the latter, the more likely conventional conflict becomes. If we focus on China as the source of our problems, the likelihood increases that our two countries will draw swords against one another, either in conventional conflict or through the modern-day economic equivalent of the Cold War. Conversely, the more we focus on changing ourselves, the more likely it is that America will be able to enact the reforms needed for our own economy and government to thrive in the twenty-first century.

COLLABORATE AND REFINE THE EXISTING MODEL

Those who would advocate for a continued engagement with China that elevates collaboration and refines the existing way our two countries have worked together over the last thirty years must acknowledge one important caveat: such a willingness is contingent on Beijing progressing in the areas of human rights, accommodating political dissent, and genuinely moving forward on becoming a responsible global stakeholder. Should China become even more belligerent in areas such as human rights or the suppression of political dissent or should the country make moves to further destabilize existing regional powers, then the willingness to continue investing in a refined model of engagement by America should decrease. Measuring China's progress in these areas is not easy, but then again neither was it easy to measure America's. Our own history is well marked by major chapters in which our actions came up well short of our ideals. It will be the same with China, perhaps even more so considering where China is coming from.

Refining today's model of engagement requires that we first acknowledge what is broken in the existing global rule set, then propose what should be done to do to fix it. Conventional free trade theory acknowledges that certain economic activities will gravitate to countries that have comparative advantages. Undeveloped countries with little in the way of natural resources or other things to trade with will need to focus their economy on providing low-cost labor to the world. Countries with higher costs but a skilled labor force will similarly focus on portions of the value chain in which higher technology skill sets are necessary. This is how global trade has always worked in the past and how it will work in the future. Trying to legislate against this sort of mobile economic activity will do nothing but slow economic growth for everyone. But this does not mean that developed economies should have approached the modern era of globalization as they did. There are lessons to be learned about how the introduction of 3 billion low-cost laborers from China and India has impacted workers across America and the European Union, and there are ideas on how to ameliorate the impact these people feel. We know now that too few Western countries were prepared to transition large segments of their economy still reliant on low to moderate skill level manufacturing into higher-value jobs. As we look forward into a future in which new and automated technologies threaten to again upend both blue- and white-collar jobs everywhere, now is a particularly good time for political thinkers and business leaders around the world to reflect carefully on the right way to think about global trade, as well as what sort of social contract may be needed in order to maintain stable societies. If Western political thinking proves unable to adapt and reimagine what it means to live in a world in which globalization and automation coexist, the likelihood that the world finds a new normal absent conflict seems low.

It bears repeating that much of the failure traditional laborers across the West are now living with can be attributed to two issues: first, simple inattention from their political leaders and second, a misunderstanding of the role of the market to help manage through periods of instability and uncertainty. As was discussed earlier in this book during the exploration of American domestic industrial policy in the nineties, during this period traditional manufacturing was treated as a redheaded step child with little effort directed toward making sure people reliant on a vibrant manufacturing economy were either protected or properly assisted as they transitioned into new parts of the economy. Free market advocates made the mistake of conflating the good a globalized world would do for business with the good it would do for individuals. We can now say with confidence that the benefits of globalization accrued more quickly to business than to people.

These are not easy refinements for American politics to make. Because America is ideologically predisposed to believe the free market is an expression of human liberty, we approach critical moments like the entry of 3 billion low-cost laborers into the global workforce with the belief that the market is the best way to sort out the winners from the losers. On this point, American thinking is right; however, it is an unfinished thought. The market's ruthless efficiency also comes at a cost, and advocates of an unfettered free market approach to globalization and automation should keep in mind that the painful shaking-out process they blindly trust has political implications and social costs attached to it as well, one of which is war. If the disaffected group is large enough, it can destabilize a nation's politics and the globalization scheme within which the modern world has been built. Conservative advocates of the free market have historically undervalued the role of government, nowhere more than in their underappreciation of how government can ease a nation's economy from one form of production to another. The refinement of our policy of engagement with China should be done in tandem with similar refinements as to the role of both government and the market as the organizing mechanisms for American life.

We need government precisely for those moments, such as the late nineties, when a very positive phenomenon—the knitting of the world together by globalization—was released to the potential detriment of many fellow citizens. Conservatives are not wrong to question what the right role of government is during these moments, as well as the practical limits to what society can afford. Government's role in moments like these may be less to directly compensate those affected (although even such conservative libertarians as Charles Murray now, in the face of fears over the instability posed by automation, support universal basic income), and more to create incentives for new sectors of the economy to grow, for entrepreneurs to take risks, for people to geographically move where the new jobs are being created, and for retraining our workforce.[3] Cosmetically, the American government took some actions along these lines. But American policy makers paid too little attention to how serious the downside economic risks of a globalized world could be; we underinvested in education and infrastructure; we too highly valued the service versus manufacturing economy; we spent our peace dividend on many of the wrong things; and both progressives and conservatives proved to be overly reliant on the idea that the market would somehow seamlessly address all of this.

One of the most important factors that would allow the U.S.-China relationship to peacefully find a new equilibrium would be an adjustment of American expectations around the outcomes of China's political and economic reforms. The simple calculus that an economically engaged China would come to look like us politically is clearly a fallacy; however, we have every reason to believe that if we continue to engage China, it will come to look much more like us than either Mao or Nixon would have ever thought possible. In the midst of our anxieties about China's accumulating power, we can easily forget that the world in general has always had similar concerns about American power. Going forward, America may well need to engage China with a more acute sense of Washington's limitations in the past. Yet such a relationship need not be one that China can manipulate to its advantage any more than Washington could once have—had it so wished—engaged China purely to America's own benefit.

IS CHINA A THREAT?

Pulling back from the unproductive and hostile attitudes toward China that have flared up in the late 2010s will not be easy. Because rebalancing our relationship will require an appetite for making major structural changes to our own political processes and economy, the easier choice will always be for Americans to believe that China represents a threat to our own power and that we should act to prevent any further ascent by China. Animated by a profound frustration not seen in the country since the thirties, a period when America danced with many of its own political demons, the United States today under Donald Trump's leadership could do more to roll back globalization than any other country in the world. This would not be without historical precedent. Henry Kissinger's most famous written work remains *A World Restored*, in which he studied the transition of power within continental Europe in the transitional decades after the Treaty of Westphalia and what the treaty says about the challenges inherent in an emerging power's confrontation of the established order and a power structure designed to perpetuate the objectives of those currently in charge. His conclusions are not comforting: "only absolute security—the neutralization of the opponent—is considered a sufficient guarantee, and thus the desire of one power for absolute security means absolute insecurity for all the other."[4]

It can be overly reductionist to argue that the rise of one great power and the decline of another inevitably breeds conflict, but this does fit within what we know about human behavior. Pundits eager to dismiss the ideas of Niall Ferguson and Graham Allison see nuanced details they believe distinguish today's U.S.-China relationship from previous moments in which the world lost its mind and went to war. But the idea that America's profound sense of loss and the mounting insecurities Middle America goes to bed with every night are only fleeting fears is badly mistaken. These fears and insecurities will all get worse as the limits of what America's current politics are able to achieve for most families come sharply into focus. These fears were only partially captured in the 2016 election. There is more to come, and what likely comes next will be even more dramatic and unpredictable than what we have seen in 2017. Should the United States determine that refining the existing model of engagement is no longer adequate, America will also blame China for problems entirely of DC's making. Four ideas will be used to rationalize blaming China: China will be put forward as the cause of America's economic struggles, Beijing will be perceived as intransigent in key areas of reform, China's efforts to pursue its own domestic priorities will be perceived not to align with international expectations, and last, the Beijing Model will be understood as a threat to America's democratic form of government, one the United States cannot allow to stand.

As is often the case, shades of truth will exist within each of these assertions; however, these insights will be obscured by our need to have an existential enemy against which we can define ourselves, draw strength from, and summon the unity that has proven so evasive since 9/11. The idea that China is the cause of our economic problems is already spreading. Bookshelves are filling up with new works on globalization and whether its forces can rightly be seen as a good or whether it needs to be somehow modified. The mere fact that this discussion intensified in the run-up to the 2016 election is proof that it is a question many Americans are asking themselves. Too often academics and policy makers remain distant from these concerns, safely ensconced in a world of ideas and not the day-to-day pressures that come with life in modern America. In addition, the perception of intransigence by Beijing will be fed by what is already happening in the South China Sea. But the most useful rationalization that will allow conflict with China to be seen as both acceptable and necessary is that the Chinese model is an affront to democracy. It is no coincidence that many of those most critical of China's economic rise are also those who make a point of dropping "Communist" into every conversation about China and its policies.

As it happens, I am writing the closing chapter of this book on a flight from Beijing to Wenzhou. In front of me are two obviously rural Chinese men on what I suspect is their first flight. They play with the seat, pushing it back and forth like a new La-Z-Boy, much to the agony of my knees. They squawk with the sort of delight that seems odd for two adult men to have, which leaves me and many of the other more urbane travelers somewhat embarrassed. Yet this is China. This new Airbus jets us to the entrepreneurially driven and newly rich Wenzhou, carrying with it many Chinese who cannot begin to fathom where their country is today, let alone where it is going. Whether our two countries can summon the strength to let these two men build new lives without upending our own, whether we can manage our own needs as Americans against those of these two men remains to be seen. If we choose the easier path of viewing them as a threat, we miss the much-greater likelihood that it will be our own actions and lack of willpower to change that has led the world to conflict.

DETERMINING THE WAY FORWARD

What determines which way we go forward, whether we rebalance or treat China as a threat? There are four strategic factors that will determine whether we blame China or dig deep and make the tough choices that will help both countries prosper. The first is which direction the American economy goes. It could well be that the reforms enacted by a Republican-led federal government lead to economic growth. But should the U.S. economy again stall or even worse have another series of structural problems similar to what happened in 2008, the likelihood that American policy toward China remains benign is slim. The second factor is what Trump could be the preamble to, both with respect to America's political soul and to how American policy orients itself to the world in general and to China specifically. The third is not within America's control; it has to do with China's internal reforms and actions toward its neighbors. Fourth is whether the new normal of a multipolar world proves itself sustainable and conflict free in ways previous eras have not. A fragmented world is one that puts the needs of more local actors above those of the world and in so doing prevents the idea of a global commons from governing what individual countries do in pursuit of self-interest.

Against all this is the pressing need for a compelling vision as to what American power means in the twenty-first century and how our ideals create opportunities for the average family. America badly needs its leaders to begin making a more vocal case for the world they envision, a world in which America can compete. Businesspeople need to make this argument from their perspective as global citizens but doubling down to incorporate the considerations of countries from which they hail and the needs of their countrymen. What businesses achieve, and the profits they are able to realize as a consequence of opening markets in the emerging world, cannot be the only factor that drives their perspective on which policies America should pursue. Business must come to care more about policies that ensure a vibrant middle class continues to exist in the home country.

Around the country American families are begging their leaders to cast a vision of the country's path forward. A morbid insecurity in the American political soul exists today, one we would do well to recognize is a cancer that could lead our country down the darkest of passages. America's insecurity could upend the historical role our country has played of being a force for good and instead cause us to believe that upending the globalized world is not only necessary but justified given China's malicious intent. Think of what America has done since 9/11, the lengths we have been willing to go to protect ourselves, the international rules we have been willing to throw away, all in pursuit of our own security.

This book was, admittedly, not the lightest of pursuits. We are on a path toward blaming China for our own mistakes. As such, we are likely to pursue wrong-headed policies designed to remedy a world we no longer believe works like we wished it would. My question to my fellow

Americans is this: will you allow yourself to be distracted by China, to blame it for problems of our own making, or will you turn your attention to the changes we need to pursue first? Changing ourselves is admittedly much harder than simply blaming China. While blaming China may be more emotionally satisfying and present immediate gratification, it is a mirage. Even if the wishes of those most hostile toward China were to be realized, the problems we live with in America would not go away; in fact, many would intensify.

Refuse to fall for the cheap thinking and illusory trap of believing our problems are of China's making. Believe that if we can change how we talk to one another and elevate our conversations accordingly, we can find a way forward. Give yourself over to the idea that America has every right to believe itself to be the ideal of human expression, but invest yourself equally in embodying the version of the American ideal you want China to be. Nothing will change China faster than tens of millions of Americans rediscovering the central truths that have defined our country and created our success for the last two hundred years.

CONCLUSION

I have never before felt this way about my own country. I can find historical comparisons to the anger we are directing toward one another or to how the growing sense of disorder around the world adds to our collective anxiety, but they offer little succor about what is to come.

Our world reeks of fear. Progressives fear America is lurching toward authoritarianism, while conservatives fear America is asleep to the dangers of excessive government, the United States' declining power and terrorism. Not only do we not share one another's fears, but we also see in the other's fears something to despise, a sense of moral or intellectual superiority that makes our fear more prescient and therefore more useful.

When fear becomes the animating principle of any society, strongmen rejoice. When societies are divided against one another, the wisdom of the moderate middle cannot be heard. When extremist positions prevent us from holding two different ideas in equal tension with one another, only brute force remains.

And yet I refuse to give in to this fear. I reject despair because I believe that as many challenges as we might face as Americans, I would rather play our hand than those dealt to any other country in the world today. While our challenges are many, they are nothing compared to those faced by China's leadership. We can still escape the trap of postmodern relativism that western Europe faces as it stares down the triple threat of antisemitism, home-grown terrorism, and right-wing nationalism. While our problem with special interests is profound and pervasive, these groups already recognize that economic fundamentalism has led to a moment of populist anger that will limit future potential profits. Our situation is eminently fixable.

We remain the world's strongest economy with the most powerful military and the most coherent—if currently strained—social contract and rule of law. Our companies and academic institutions remain engines of innovation. We are the envy of all, and at the same time we are a source of extreme confusion and anxiety by those watching us from the outside in.

It is entirely within our abilities to fight the fear, to listen to those we disagree with, and to again find ways in which we channel the legitimate concerns of those on both sides of the political aisle. And here is the simple and elegant truth uniquely available to us as Americans: no country in the history of mankind has ever given its people more say, more representation, or more influence in the affairs of its government than ours.

And so, ask—even fight—for change, if you will. But do so only after you change how you think, how you talk about those you disagree with, and how you act in society.

How do we make these changes? Refuse to consume outrage. Put yourself on a media diet. Watch less and read more. Learn from those who make an honest effort to intelligently evaluate both sides of an issue, and reject those who are reliable shills for either candidate. Look for complexity and nuance, even if it is not satisfying.

Believe that those you disagree with are working in good faith. Look for what is good, and pay particular attention to those who offer up an idea of where we might go together without hurting others. Intentionally reach out to someone you know who disagrees with your politics, and require from yourself a conversation about politics that sheds more light than heat. Reward independent thinkers and reject extremists.

Do these things and vote. Stop looking for a messiah who can be sent to DC to solve our problems. We are our best problem solvers. We will never require better conduct from our politicians until we require the same from ourselves.

When Congress is incapable of civility and compromise, we are the cause. When empty personalities become viable political candidates, it is because we have utterly and entirely embraced the politics of personality over anything that could be called a shadow of substance. When politicians speak empty phrases, bereft of anything that provokes their own supporters to think and wrestle with the complexities of modern life, we have our own consumption of outraged political TV to thank.

For all of its past and present flaws, American democracy is beautiful. It expresses the best version yet for how everyone, not just the wealthy and entitled, can participate in their government and culture.

Reject fear.

Refuse to blame China for problems that are wholly our making.

NOTES

1. AFRAID OF CHINA?

1. Gass, "China to Trump."
2. Gass, "Trump: We Can't Continue."
3. Sanders, Senate Speech.
4. Merica and Bradner, "Hillary Clinton."
5. Rohrabacher, Floor Speech in Opposition to Foreign Aid to Communist China.
6. Benjamin Haas, "Steve Bannon: 'We're going to war in the South China Sea . . . no doubt,'" *The Guardian*, February 1, 2017, https://www.theguardian.com/us -news/2017/feb/02/steve-bannon-donald-trump-war-south-china-sea-no-doubt.
7. Trump, Foreign Policy Speech.
8. Macha, "U.S.-China Relations."
9. Fromkin, *Europe's Last Summer*, 295–96.
10. Barnett, "Why China Matters to You," 58–65.
11. Ryan, *On Politics*, 63.

2. THE DRAGON SLAYER'S CHINA

1. Mark McDonald, "New Survey Finds U.S. Concerns over a Rising China," *New York Times*, June 27, 2012, http://rendezvous.blogs.nytimes.com/2012/06 /27/new-survey-finds-u-s-concerns-over-a-rising-china/.
2. Eric X. Li, "Why China's Political Model is Superior," *New York Times*, February 16, 2012, http://www.nytimes.com/2012/02/16/opinion/why-chinas-political -model-is-superior.html.
3. Friedberg, *A Contest for Supremacy*, xii–xiv.

4. Jonathan Watts, "China Olympic Crackdown Grows," *The Guardian*, June 17, 2008, https://www.theguardian.com/world/2008/jun/18/china.olympicgames2008.

5. Tom Phillips, "A Human Rights Activist, A Secret Prison and a Tale from Xi Jinping's New China," *The Guardian*, January 2, 2017, https://www.theguardian.com/world/2017/jan/03/human-rights-activist-peter-dahlin-secret-black-prison-xi-jinpings-new-china.

6. Chang Ping, "In Xi Jinping's Crackdown on Civil Society, Even Women's Rights Activists Aren't Spared," *South China Morning Post*, March 16, 2015, http://www.scmp.com/comment/insight-opinion/article/1739150/xi-jinpings-crackdown-civil-society-even-womens-rights.

7. Griffiths, "Report: China Still Harvesting."

8. Emily Rauhala and Simon Denyer, "Pursuing Critics, China Reaches Across Borders: and Nobody Is Stopping It," *Washington Post*, January 26, 2016, https://www.washingtonpost.com/world/asia_pacific/pursuing-critics-china-reaches-across-borders-and-nobody-is-stopping-it/2016/01/26/cd4959dc-6793-473f-8b74-6cbac3f46422_story.html.

9. Edward Wong, "Pastor in China Who Resisted Cross Removal Gets 14 Years in Prison," *New York Times*, February 26, 2016, http://www.nytimes.com/2016/02/27/world/asia/china-zhejiang-christians-pastor-crosses.html.

10. Stuart Leavenworth, "Christian Church Leader Jailed in Chinese Human Rights Crackdown," *The Guardian*, August 3, 2016, https://www.theguardian.com/world/2016/aug/03/christian-church-leader-hu-shigen-jailed-chinese-human-rights-crackdown.

11. Tiezzi, "Report: To Reach Mars."

12. Navarro, *The Coming China Wars*, 1.

13. Gardels, "China vs. America."

14. Osman, "The Fall of Hosni Mubarak."

15. Bush and Scowcroft, *A World Transformed*, 179.

16. Clinton, The President's News Conference.

17. Mann, *The China Fantasy*, 10.

3. THE PANDA HUGGER'S CHINA

1. Mingfu, "The World Is Too Important."

2. Kuo, "Why Are So Many First-Generation."

3. Estimates for this famine range, but the most recent and widely accepted survey of Chinese data sources is Yang Jisheng's *Tombstone: The Great Chinese Famine*,

1958–1962 (New York: Farrar, Straus and Giroux, 2008). Here he supports the conclusion that approximately 36 million Chinese died during this period due to food shortages.

4. Readers who want to know more should seek out Bruce Elleman's *Taiwan Straits: Crisis in Asia and the Role of the U.S. Navy* (Lanham MD: Rowman and Littlefield, 2014).

5. Ariel Tian, "Mao's 'Nuclear Mass Extinction Speech' Aired on Chinese TV," *Epoch Times*, April 2, 2013, https://www.theepochtimes.com/maos-nuclear -mass-extinction-speech-aired-on-chinese-tv_4758.html.

6. "The E.R. Presents: Lawfare and FP's Bar Review Live," November 7, 2016, in *Foreign Policy's The Editor's Roundtable Podcast*.

7. Readers may wish to compile their own list here: https://en.wikipedia.org /wiki/List_of_wars_1500%e2%80%931799.

8. Friedberg, *A Contest for Supremacy*, 72.

9. Woody, "Video Shows Chinese."

10. Valentino , *Final Solutions*, 88.

11. Maddison, "The West and the Rest in the World Economy."

12. "What Economist Arvind Subramanian Thinks of 'China 2030," *Wall Street Journal*, March 2, 2012, https://blogs.wsj.com/chinarealtime/2012/03/02/what -economist-arvind-subramanian-thinks-of-china-2030/.

13. Lin and Liu, "Trends of Population Growth."

14. Jackson, "The Aging of China."

15. Devichand, "China."

16. Kaneda, "China's Concern Over Population."

17. Shobert, "Asia Rolling Headlong to Disaster."

18. Shobert, "Asia Rolling Headlong to Disaster."

19. Benjamin Haas, "More than 100 Chinese Cities Now above 1 Million People," *The Guardian*, March 20, 2017, https://www.theguardian.com/cities/2017/mar /20/china-100-cities-populations-bigger-liverpool.

4. COLLIDING WORLDVIEWS

1. "The Opening of China."

2. Goldfarb, "The Nation Asks 'Why."

3. Weisberg, "Republicans, Democrats, and China."

4. Nixon, "Asia After Viet Nam."

5. Norris, "Quemoy and Matsu."

6. Stanley Michalak, "Bill Clinton's Adventures in the Jungle of Foreign Policy," *USA Today*, March 1995, https://www.questia.com/magazine/1g1-16805672/bill -clinton-s-adventures-in-the-jungle-of-foreign.

7. Doug Bandow, "Demonizing China for Political Profit," *Huffington Post*, http://www.huffingtonpost.com/doug-bandow/demonizing-china-for-poli _b_1972881.html.

8. Diamond, "Trump."

9. Steven Mufson, "Is Obama's Iran Overture like Nixon's Opening to China?," March 14, 2015, https://www.washingtonpost.com/business/economy/is-obamas -iran-overture-like-nixons-opening-to-china/2015/03/13/09d5ff98-c7fd-11e4 -a199–6cb5e63819d2_story.html?utm_term=.dda17a435a41.

10. Julian Borger, "Barack Obama: Administration Willing to Talk to Iran 'without Preconditions,'" *The Guardian*, January 21, 2009, https://www.theguardian.com /world/2009/jan/21/barack-obama-iran-negotiations.

11. Mearsheimer and Walt, "An Unnecessary War."

12. Taylor, "Rising Protests in China."

5. AMERICA'S ECONOMIC INSECURITY

1. Scott, "Rick Santorum."

2. American Society for Microbiology, National Institutes of Health FY 2018 Appropriations Statement.

3. Krugman, "In Praise of Cheap Labor."

4. Friedman, *The World Is Flat*, 46.

5. "Globalization: The Challenge to America: Computers and the Internet Have Made the World a Much Smaller Place—and Brought Foreign Competition Right to America's Doorstep."

6. Prestowitz, "Free Trade Is Dead."

7. Pollack, "Stagnant Wages, Rising Inequality."

8. Censky, "How the Middle Class."

9. Censky, "How the Middle Class."

10. Shobert, "Congress Hits Anti-China Drum."

11. Pisano and Shih, "Restoring American Competitiveness."

12. Breznitz, *Innovation and the State*, 191.

13. Denning, "Amazon Can't Make a Kindle."

14. Denning, "Amazon Can't Make a Kindle."

15. Rattner, "The Secret of Germany's Success."

16. Office of the United States Trade Representative, "The People's Republic of China."

17. Office of the United States Trade Representative, "The People's Republic of China."

6. OUR PLACE IN THE WORLD

1. Allen, "Don't Do Stupid Sh— [Stuff]."

2. Goldberg, "Obama Doctrine."

3. Rosenberger, "Can the U.S.-Japan Alliance."

4. Alison Smale and Steven Erlanger, "Merkel, After Discordant G-7 Meeting, Is Looking Past Trump," *New York Times*, May 28, 2017, https://www.nytimes.com /2017/05/28/world/europe/angela-merkel-trump-alliances-g7-leaders.html?_r=0.

5. Greg R. Lawson, "How Trump Could Make American Foreign Policy Great Again," *The Hill*, April 10, 2016, http://thehill.com/blogs/pundits-blog/international /279318-how-trump-could-make-american-foreign-policy-great-again.

6. Short, *Mao*, 423.

7. Tim Weiner, "Stalin-Mao Alliance Was Uneasy, Newly Released Papers Show," *New York Times*, December 10, 1995, http://www.nytimes.com/1995/12/10/world /stalin-mao-alliance-was-uneasy-newly-released-papers-show.html.

8. Harry Schwartz, "Khrushchev-Mao Clashes on Party Issues Revealed," *New York Times International*, February 12, 1961, https://partners.nytimes.com/library /world/asia/021261mao-khrushchev.html.

9. MacMillan, *Nixon and Mao*, 134.

10. MacMillan, *Nixon and Mao*, 134.

11. Roach and McNamara, "Defending Defense."

12. Klein, "The Peace Dividend."

13. Klein, "The Peace Dividend."

14. Bill Maher, interview with Richard Trumka, October 9, 2011, https://www .youtube.com/watch?v=TJs3Vy0jCL0.

15. Klein, "The Peace Dividend."

16. Moses, "'We Are the World,'" 2.

17. Glass, "Bush Announces Launch."

18. "Neoconservative Think Tank."

19. Jon Ward, "Big Government Gets Bigger," *Washington Times*, October 19, 2008, http://www.washingtontimes.com/news/2008/oct/19/big-government -gets-bigger/.

20. Frum, "The Republican Waterloo."
21. Burns and Jennifer Medina, "The Single Payer Party? Democrats Shift Left on Healthcare," *New York Times*, June 3, 2017, https://www.nytimes.com/2017 /06/03/us/democrats-universal-health-care-single-payer-party.html.
22. Glueck, "Cruz Pledges Relentless Bombing."
23. "Why Do So Many People Hate Obama?"
24. Sager, "Stop Calling Obama a Liberal."
25. Bennet, "Obama Is No Liberal."
26. Chris Cillizza, "Is Barack Obama the Most Liberal President Ever?," *Washington Post*, February 4, 2014, https://www.washingtonpost.com/news/the-fix /wp/2014/02/04/is-barack-obama-the-most-liberal-president-ever/?utm_term =.e0f92861122c.
27. Sirota, "Obama Isn't Weak."
28. Rose, "What Obama Gets Right."

7. THE AMORPHOUS THREAT OF TERRORISM

1. Plotz, "What Does Osama bin Laden Want?"
2. Engelhardt, "14 Years after 9/11."
3. Gavel, "Linda Bilmes on the U.S."
4. Bilmes, "The Financial Legacy of Iraq and Afghanistan."
5. Chris Alcantara, "45 Years of Terrorist Attacks in Europe, Visualized," *Washington Post*, July 17, 2017, https://www.washingtonpost.com/graphics/world/a -history-of-terrorism-in-europe/.
6. Burrough, "The Bombings of America."
7. Ben-David, "Europe's Shifting Immigration Dynamic," 15–24.
8. "Migrant Crisis."
9. Hacket, "5 Facts about the Muslim Population in Europe."
10. Mosher and Gould, "How Likely Are Foreign Terrorists to Kill Americans?"
11. Mosher and Gould, "How Likely Are Foreign Terrorists to Kill Americans?"
12. Mueller and Stewart, *Chasing Ghosts*, 252–53.
13. William Safire, "If You Break It . . . ," *New York Times*, October 17, 2004, http:// www.nytimes.com/2004/10/17/magazine/if-you-break-it.html.
14. "Bush: Don't Wait for Mushroom Cloud."

8. AMERICA'S DYSFUNCTIONAL SYSTEM

1. Frank, *Listen Liberal*, 68.

2. Chen Chenchen, "Red Dawn Shows Nostalgia for Cold War Mindset," *Global Times*, November 27, 2012, http://www.globaltimes.cn/content/746657.shtml.

3. Wake Up Wal-Mart, "Wal-Mart: The Real Story."

4. Dobbs, "Dangerous Imports from China."

5. David Moye, "Kid Rock Blasts China-Made BBQ Grills Because 'Murica," *Huffington Post*, March 13, 2017, http://www.huffingtonpost.com/entry/kid-rock-blasts-grills_us_58c70f74e4b0598c6698ff80.

6. Congressional Budget Office, "Understanding the Long-Term Budget Outlook."

7. Mysak, "Meredith Whitney Wins."

8. Katie Allen, "Are the Wheels about to Fall Off the Credit Gravy Train?," *The Guardian*, April 8, 2017, https://www.theguardian.com/money/2017/apr/08/consumer-debt-loans-credit-cards-bank-of-england.

9. Cosgrove-Mather, "Americans Have Negative Savings Rate."

10. Gretchen Morgenson, "Given a Shovel, Americans Dig Deeper into Debt," *New York Times*, July 20, 2008, http://www.nytimes.com/2008/07/20/business/20debt.html.

11. Bartlett, "Fiscal Responsibility Requires Higher Taxes."

12. Ward, "U.S. Teeters on Double-Dip Recession."

13. Scutt, "China Is Selling US Government Debt."

14. "U.S. Debt: How Big Is It and Who Owns It?," *The Guardian*, https://www.theguardian.com/news/datablog/2011/jul/15/us-debt-how-big-who-owns.

15. Fallows, "The Tragedy of the American Military."

16. American Society of Civil Engineers, 2017 Infrastructure Report Card.

17. Fallows, "The $1.4 Trillion Question."

18. Zakaria, *The Post-American World*, 139.

19. Fallows, "The $1.4 Trillion Question."

9. WHEN WAR IS A RATIONAL CHOICE

1. Buruma, "Are China and the United States Headed for War?"

2. Karlin, "Prophets of the Great War."

3. Snyder, *On Tyranny*, 12–13.

4. Jackson and Morelli, "The Reasons for Wars," 9.

5. Fromkin, *Europe's Last Summer*, 295–96.

6. Allison, *Destined for War*, vii.

7. Mandelbaum, *The Frugal Superpower*, excerpt quoted in "On a Budget."

8. Mandelbaum, *The Frugal Superpower*, 124.

9. Stoessinger, *Why Nations Go To War*, 391.

10. TWO PATHS FORWARD

1. Rachman, "The End of the Win-Win."
2. Tom Phillips, "Donald Trump and China on Dangerous Collision Course, Say Experts," *The Guardian*, February 6, 2017, https://www.theguardian.com/us -news/2017/feb/07/donald-trump-and-china-military-confrontation-dangerous -collision-course-experts.
3. Charles Murray, "A Guaranteed Income for Every American," *Wall Street Journal*, June 3, 2016, https://www.wsj.com/articles/a-guaranteed-income-for-every -american-1464969586.
4. Kissinger, *A World Restored*, 2.

BIBLIOGRAPHY

Allen, Mike. "Don't Do Stupid Sh— [Stuff]." *Politico*, June 1, 2014. www.politico
.com/story/2014/ 06/dont-do-stupid-shit-president-obama-white-house-107293.

American Society for Microbiology. National Institutes of Health FY 2018 Appropriations Statement. *American Society for Microbiology*, February 24, 2017. www
.asm.org/index.php/ statements-and-testimony/item/6041-nih-fy2018.

American Society of Civil Engineers. 2017 Infrastructure Report Card. *American
Society of Civil Engineers*. www.infrastructurereportcard.org/.

Barnett, Thomas. "Why China Matters to You." *Good Magazine*, May/June 2008, 58–65.

Bartlett, Bruce. "Fiscal Responsibility Requires Higher Taxes." *Forbes*, September 25,
2009. www.forbes.com/2009/09/24/fiscal-spending-taxes-opinions-columnists
-bruce-bartlett.html.

Ben-David, Esther. "Europe's Shifting Immigration Dynamic." *Middle East Quarterly*,
Spring 2009: 15–24. www.meforum.org/2107/europe-shifting-immigration
-dynamic.

Bennet, James. "Obama Is No Liberal." *The Atlantic*, July/August 2010. www
.theatlantic.com/magazine/archive/2010/07/obama-is-no-liberal/308157/.

Bilmes, Linda. "The Financial Legacy of Iraq and Afghanistan: How Wartime
Spending Discussions will Constrain Future National Security Budgets." HKS
Faculty Research Working Paper Series RWP13–006, Harvard Kennedy School,
Cambridge MA, March 2013. https://research.hks.harvard.edu/publications
/workingpapers/citation.aspx?PubId=8956&type=wpn.

Breznitz, Daniel. *Innovation and the State*. New Haven CT: Yale University Press, 2007.

Burrough, Bryan. "The Bombings of America that We Forgot." *Time Magazine*,
September 20, 2016. http://time.com/4501670/bombings-of-america-burrough/.

Buruma, Ian. "Are China and the United States Headed for War?" *New Yorker*, June 19, 2017. www.newyorker.com/magazine/2017/06/19/are-china-and-the-united-states-headed-for-war.

"Bush: Don't Wait for Mushroom Cloud." CNN, October 8, 2002. http://www.cnn.com/2002/allpolitics/10/07/bush.transcript/index.html?_s=pm:allpolitics.

Bush, George, and Brent Scowcroft. *A World Transformed*. New York: Vintage, 1999.

Censky, Annalyn. "How the Middle Class Became the Underclass." CNN *Money*, February 16, 2011. http://money.cnn.com/2011/02/16/news/economy/middle_class/.

Clinton, William J. The President's News Conference. Speech, May 26, 1994. American Presidency Project. www.presidency.ucsb.edu/ws/?pid=50241.

Congressional Budget Office. "Understanding the Long-Term Budget Outlook." Congressional Budget Office, July 9, 2015. www.cbo.gov/publication/50316.

Cosgrove-Mather, Bootie. "Americans Have Negative Savings Rate." CBS, February 7, 2006. www.cbsnews.com/news/americans-have-negative-savings-rate/.

Denning, Steve. "Amazon Can't Make a Kindle in the USA." *Forbes*, August 17, 2011. www.forbes.com/sites/stevedenning/2011/08/17/why-amazon-cant-make-a-kindle-in-the-usa/#3d57f8ff18d0.

Devichand, Mukul. "China: Growing Old before It Can Grow Rich?" BBC, May 17, 2012. www.bbc.com/news/world-asia-china-18091107.

Diamond, Jeremy. "Trump: We Can't Continue to Allow China to Rape Our Country." CNN, May 2, 2016. www.cnn.com/2016/05/01/politics/donald-trump-china-rape/index.html.

Dobbs, Lou. "Dangerous Imports from China." CNN, www.youtube.com/watch?v=3hhxJhQaOsQ.

Engelhardt, Tom. "14 Years after 9/11, the War on Terror Is Accomplishing Everything bin Laden Hoped It Would." *The Nation*, September 2015.

"The E.R. Presents: Lawfare and FP's Bar Review Live." November 7, 2016. In *Foreign Policy's The Editor's Roundtable*, podcast.

Fallows, James. "The $1.4 Trillion Question." *The Atlantic*, January/February 2008. www.theatlantic.com/magazine/archive/2008/01/the-14-trillion-question/306582/.

———. "The Tragedy of the American Military." *The Atlantic*, January/February 2015. www.theatlantic.com/magazine/archive/2015/01/the-tragedy-of-the-american-military/383516/.

Frank, Thomas. *Listen, Liberal: Or, What Ever Happened to the Party of the People?*. New York: Metropolitan, 2016.

Friedberg, Aaron L. *A Contest for Supremacy: China, America, and the Struggle for Mastery in Asia*. New York: W. W. Norton, 2011.

Friedman, Tom. *The World Is Flat.* New York: Farrar, Straus and Giroux, 2005.

Fromkin, David. *Europe's Last Summer: Who Started the Great War in 1914?* New York: Knopf, 2004.

Frum, David. "The Republican Waterloo." *The Atlantic*, March 24, 2017. www .theatlantic.com/politics/archive/2017/03/the-republican-waterloo/520833/.

Gardels, Nathan. "China vs. America: Which Government Model Will Triumph?" *Christian Science Monitor*, January 27, 2010. www.csmonitor.com/Commentary /Global-Viewpoint/2010/0127/China-vs.-America-Which-government-model -will-triumph.

Gass, Nick. "China to Trump: We're Not Stealing American Jobs." *Politico*, June 17, 2015. www.politico.com/story/2015/06/donald-trump-china-jobs-119099.

———. "Trump: We Can't Continue to Let China Rape Our Country." *Politico*, May 2, 2016. www.politico.com/blogs/2016-gop-primary-live-updates-and-results /2016/05/trump-china-rape-america-222689.

Gavel, Doug. "Linda Bilmes on the U.S. Engagement in Iraq and Afghanistan: 'The Most Expensive Wars in U.S. History.'" *Harvard Kennedy School of Government*, March 28, 2013. www.hks.harvard.edu/news-events/news/articles/bilmes-iraq -afghan-war-cost-wp.

Gilley, Bruce. *China's Democratic Future: How It Will Happen and Where It Will Lead.* New York: Columbia University Press, 2004.

Glass, Andrew. "Bush Announces Launch of Operation Iraqi Freedom, March 19, 2003." *Politico*, March 18, 2017. www.politico.com/story/2017/03/bush-announces -launch-of-operation-iraqi-freedom-march-19-2003-236134.

"Globalization: The Challenge to America: Computers and the Internet Have Made the World a Much Smaller Place—and Brought Foreign Competition Right to America's Doorstep." *Free Library*, 2005. www.thefreelibrary.com /Globalization%3a+the+challenge+to+America%3a+computers+and+the +Internet . . .-a0137859996.

Glueck, Katie. "Cruz Pledges Relentless Bombing to Destroy ISIL." *Politico*, December 5, 2015. www.politico.com/story/2015/12/cruz-isil-bombing-216454.

Goldberg, Jeffrey. "The Obama Doctrine." *The Atlantic*, April 2016. www.theatlantic .com/magazine/archive/2016/04/the-obama-doctrine/471525/.

Goldfarb, Michael. "The Nation Asks 'Why Can't Republicans Be More Like Nixon?'" *Weekly Standard*, April 13, 2007. www.weeklystandard.com/the-nation -asks-why-cant-republicans-be-more-like-nixon/article/19269.

Graham, Allison. *Destined for War: Can American and China Escape Thucydides's Trap?* Boston: Houghton Mifflin Harcourt, 2017.

Griffiths, James. "Report: China Still Harvesting Organs from Prisoners at a Massive Scale." CNN, June 24, 2016. www.cnn.com/2016/06/23/asia/china-organ -harvesting/.

Hacket, Conrad. "5 Facts about the Muslim Population in Europe." *Pew Research Center*, July 19, 2016. www.pewresearch.org/fact-tank/2016/07/19/5-facts-about -the-muslim-population-in-europe/.

Jackson, Matthew, and Massimo Morelli. "The Reasons for Wars—an Updated Survey." *Stanford*. http://web.stanford.edu/~jacksonm/war-overview.pdf.

Jackson, Richard. "The Aging of China." CSIS, April 20, 2010. www.csis.org/analysis /aging-china-0.

Kaneda, Toshiko. "China's Concern over Population Aging and Health." *Population Reference Bureau*, 2006. www.prb.org/Publications/Articles/2006 /ChinasConcernOverPopulationAgingandHealth.aspx.

Karlin, Anatoly. "Prophets of the Great War: Friedrich Engels, Ivan Bloch, and Pyotr Durnovo." *Anatoly Karlin* (blog), April 2010. http://akarlin.com/2010 /05/great-war-prophets/.

Kissinger, Henry. *A World Restored*. Williamsville: Mariner Books, 1973.

Klein, Joe. *Primary Colors*. New York: Random House, 2006.

Klein, Lawrence R. "The Peace Dividend." Paper presented at meetings of the Latin American and Caribbean Economic Association, Costa Rica, November 2004.

Krugman, Paul. "In Praise of Cheap Labor." *Slate*, March 21, 1997. www.slate.com /articles/business/the_dismal_science/1997/03/in_praise_of_cheap_labor.html.

Kuo, Kaiser. "Why Are So Many First-Generation Chinese Immigrants Supporting Donald Trump?" SupChina, November 3, 2016. supchina.com/2016/11/03/many -first-generation-chinese-immigrants-supporting-donald-trump/.

Lin, F., and J. Liu. "Trends of Population Growth in China: Maximum Number Will Exceed 1.5 Billion." *China Population Today* 13, no. 1 (Feb. 1996): 16–17.

Macha, Jonathan. "US-China Relations: Attitude and Attitudes." *The Diplomat*, November 2014. thediplomat.com/2014/11/us-china-relations-attitude-and -attitudes/.

MacMillan, Margaret. *Nixon and Mao: The Week that Changed the World*. New York: Random House, 2007.

Maddison, Angus. "The West and the Rest in the World Economy: 1000–2030, Maddisonian and Malthusian Interpretations." *World Economics* 9, no. 4 (2008): 75–99. www.scribd.com/document/115598688/Angus-Maddison-The-West-and -the-Rest-in-the-World-Economy-1000-2030.

Mandelbaum, Michael. *The Frugal Superpower: America's Global Leadership in a Cash-Strapped Era*. New York: PublicAffairs, 2010.

Mann, James. *The China Fantasy: Why Capitalism Will Not Bring Democracy to China*. New York: Viking, 2008.

Merica, Dan, and Eric Bradner. "Hillary Clinton Comes out against TPP Trade Deal." CNN, October 7, 2015. www.cnn.com/2015/10/07/politics/hillary-clinton -opposes-tpp/index.html.

"Migrant Crisis: Migration to Europe Explained in Seven Charts." BBC, March 4, 2016. www.bbc.com/news/world-europe-34131911.

Mingfu, Liu. "The World Is Too Important to Be Left to America," trans. Kathy Gilsinan. *The Atlantic*, June 4, 2015.

Moses, Jeremy. "'We Are the World': Cosmopolitanism, Neo-Conservatism, and Global Humanity." Paper presented at the Global Conference on Pluralism, Inclusion, and Citizenship, Salzburg, November 2007. https://ir.canterbury.ac.nz /bitstream/handle/10092/4958/12610076_pic%20paper%202007%20-%20jeremy %20moses.pdf?sequence=1&isAllowed=y.

Mosher, David, and Skye Gould. "How Likely are Foreign Terrorists to Kill Americans? The Odds May Surprise You." *Business Insider*, January 31, 2017, www .businessinsider.com/death-risk-statistics-terrorism-disease-accidents-2017-1.

Mueller, John, and Mark Stewart. *Chasing Ghosts: The Policing of Terrorism*. Oxford: Oxford University Press, 2016.

Mysak, Joe. "Meredith Whitney Wins if We Lose Meaning of Default." *Bloomberg*, July 24, 2011. www.bloomberg.com/view/articles/2011-07-25/meredith-whitney -wins-if-we-lose-meaning-of-default-joe-mysak.

Navarro, Peter. *The Coming China Wars*. Upper Saddle River NJ: FT Press, 2007.

"Neoconservative Think Tank Influence on US Policies: 1965, Former RAND Analyst Gathers Young, Nascent Neoconservatives." *History Commons*. www .historycommons.org/timeline.jsp?timeline=neoconinfluence.

Nixon, Richard. "Asia after Viet Nam." *Foreign Affairs*, October 1967.

Norris, Robert B. "Quemoy and Matsu: A Historical Footnote Revisited." *American Diplomacy*, November 2010. www.unc.edu/depts/diplomat/item/2010/0912 /comm/norris_quemoymatsu.html.

Office of the United States Trade Representative. "The People's Republic of China: US-China Trade Facts." Office of the United States Trade Representative. https:// ustr.gov/countries-regions/china-mongolia-taiwan/peoples-republic-china.

"On a Budget, U.S. Faces World as 'Frugal Superpower.'" *NPR Books*, August 22, 2010. https://www.npr.org/templates/story/story.php?storyId=129322191.

"The Opening of China." Richard Nixon Foundation, January 18, 2017. www
.nixonfoundation.org/exhibit/the-opening-of-china/.

Osman, Tarek. "The Fall of Hosni Mubarak." *Cairo Review of Global Affairs*, July 23,
2012. www.thecairoreview.com/tahrir-forum/the-fall-of-mubarak/.

Pisano, Gary, and Willy Shih. "Restoring American Competitiveness." *Harvard
Business Review*, July–August 2009. https://hbr.org/2009/07/restoring-american
-competitiveness.

Plotz, David. "What Does Osama bin Laden Want?" *Slate*, September 14, 2011. www
.slate.com/articles/news_and_politics/assessment/2001/09/what_does_osama
_bin_laden_want.html.

Pollack, Ethan. "Stagnant Wages, Rising Inequality." EPI Policy Center. www
.epipolicycenter.org/blm-stagnant_wages_and_rising_inequality.pdf.

Prestowitz, Clyde. "Free Trade Is Dead." *Washington Monthly*, June/July/August
2016. washingtonmonthly.com/magazine/junejulyaug-2016/free-trade-is-dead/.

Rachman, Gideon. "The End of the Win-Win World." *Foreign Policy*, January 24,
2012. http://foreignpolicy.com/2012/01/24/the-end-of-the-win-win-world/.

Rattner, Steven. "The Secret of Germany's Success: What Europe's Manufacturing
Powerhouse can Teach America." *Foreign Affairs*, July/August 2011. https://
www.foreignaffairs.com/articles/germany/2011-06-16/secrets-germanys-success.

Roach, Morgan Lorraine, and Sally McNamara. "Defending Defense: Setting the
Record Straight on U.S. Military Spending Requirements." Heritage Foundation, October 14, 2010. www.heritage.org/defense/report/defending-defense
-setting-the-record-straight-us-military-spending-requirements.

Rohrabacher, Dana. Floor Speech in Opposition to Foreign Aid to Communist
China. May 16, 2012. https://rohrabacher.house.gov/rohrabachers-floor-speech
-opposition-foreign-aid-communist-china.

Rose, Gideon. "What Obama Gets Right." *Foreign Affairs*, September/October 2015.
www.foreignaffairs.com/articles/what-obama-gets-right.

Rosenberger, Laura. "Can the U.S.-Japan Alliance Survive Trump?" *Foreign Policy*,
February 9, 2017. http://foreignpolicy.com/2017/02/09/can-the-u-s-japan-alliance
-survive-trump/.

Ryan, Alan. *On Politics: Book One*. New York: Liveright Publishing Corporation, 2012.

Sager, Josh. "Stop Calling Obama a Liberal." *The Progressive Cynic*, March 20, 2014.
https://theprogressivecynic.com/2014/03/20/stop-calling-obama-a-liberal/.

Sanders, Bernie. Senate Speech by Sen. Bernie Sanders on Unfettered Free Trade.
Speech, October 12, 2011. Bernie Sanders: U.S. Senator for Vermont. www

.sanders.senate.gov/newsroom/press-releases/senate-speech-by-sen-bernie
-sanders-on-unfettered-free-trade.

Scott, Dylan. "Rick Santorum: Gay Marriage Hurts the Economy." *Talking Points Memo*, June 20, 2014. http://talkingpointsmemo.com/livewire/rick-santorum
-gay-marriage-economy.

Scutt, David. "China Is Selling US Government Debt." *Business Insider*, February 16, 2016. www.businessinsider.com/china-is-selling-us-government-debt-2016-2.

Shobert, Benjamin. "Asia Rolling Headlong to Disaster." *Asia Times*, July 2, 2011. www.atimes.com/atimes/Global_Economy/mg02dj02.html.

———. "Congress Hits Anti-China Drum." *Asia Times*, August 11, 2012. www.atimes
.com/atimes/China_Business/nh11cb01.html.

Short, Philip. *Mao: A Life*. London: Henry Holt, 2000.

Sirota, David. "Obama Isn't Weak (He Just Isn't a Liberal)." *Salon*, August 5, 2011. www.salon.com/2011/08/05/obama_fdr_debt_ceiling/.

Snyder, Timothy. *On Tyranny: Twenty Lessons from the Twentieth Century*. London: Vintage, 2017.

Stoessinger, John G. *Why Nations Go to War*. Belmont: Wadsworth, 2011.

Taylor, Alan. "Rising Protests in China." *The Atlantic*, February 17, 2012. www
.theatlantic.com/photo/2012/02/rising-protests-in-china/100247/.

Tiezzi, Shannon. "Report: To Reach Mars, NASA Must Work with China." *The Diplomat*, June 2014. http://thediplomat.com/2014/06/report-to-reach-mars
-nasa-must-work-with-china/.

Mearsheimer, John J., and Stephen M. Walt. "An Unnecessary War." *Foreign Policy*. November 3, 2009. http://foreignpolicy.com/2009/11/03/an-unnecessary-war-2/.

Trump, Donald J. Foreign Policy Speech. April 27, 2016. *New York Times*. www
.nytimes.com/2016/04/28/us/politics/transcript-trump-foreign-policy.html.

———. *Great Again: How to Fix Our Crippled America*. New York: Threshold Editions, 2016.

Valentino, Benjamin A. *Final Solutions: Mass Killing and Genocide in the Twentieth Century*. Ithaca NY: Cornell University Press, 2005.

Wake Up Wal-Mart. "Wal-Mart: The Real Story." March 24, 2008. https://www
.youtube.com/watch?v=atu-Whq8isY.

Ward, Kenric. "U.S. Teeters on Double-Dip Recession." *Sunshine State News*, October 9, 2011. www.sunshinestatenews.com/story/us-teeters-double-dip-recession
-florida-already-feeling-it.

Weisberg, Jacob. "Republicans, Democrats, and China: On Human Rights, Both Parties Talk the Talk but Don't Wok the Wok." *Slate*, June 13, 1998. www

.slate.com/articles/news_and_politics/strange_bedfellow/1998/06/republicans _democrats_and_china.html.

"Why Do So Many People Hate Obama?" *Beliefnet*. www.beliefnet.com/news /articles/why-is-obama-hated.aspx.

Woody, Christopher. "Video Shows Chinese and Indian Troops Clashing with Stones High along Their Border in the Himalayas." *Business Insider*, August 20, 2017. www.businessinsider.com/video-of-chinese-indian-troops-fighting -with-stones-at-himalaya-border-2017-8.

Zakaria, Fareed. *The Post-American World.* New York: W. W. Norton, 2011.

INDEX